To Eileen
Have Joy Expressing Your Inner Light

DRAWING
the LIGHT
from
WITHIN

DRAWING the LIGHT from WITHIN

Keys to Awaken Your Creative Power

JUDITH CORNELL

Foreword by
Georg Feuerstein, Ph.D.

THIS PUBLICATION WAS MADE POSSIBLE WITH THE
ASSISTANCE OF THE KERN FOUNDATION

Quest Books
Theosophical Publishing House

Wheaton, Illinois ♦ Madras, India

To My Divine Mother

The Theosophical Publishing House
P.O. Box 270
Wheaton, IL 60189-0270

A publication of the Theosophical Publishing House,
a department of the Theosophical Society in America

Library of Congress Cataloging-in-Publication Data

Cornell, Judith
Drawing the light from within: keys to awaken your creative power
/ Judith Cornell.
p.   cm.
"A publication supported by the Kern Foundation."
"Quest books."
Originally published: New York: Prentice Hall, 1990.
Includes bibliographical references. With new pref.
ISBN 0-8356-0756-9
1. Creative ability—Problems, exercises, etc.   2. Painting—Psychological aspects—Problems, exercises, etc.
3. Drawing, Psychology of—Problems, exercises, etc.   I. Title.
[BF408.C665   1997]
153.3′5—dc21
96-40111
CIP

Black-and-white artwork photographed by Scott Hess
Book design by Robert Bull Design

6 5 4 3 2 1 * 97 98 99 00 01 02

Printed in Hong Kong by Palace Press International

ACKNOWLEDGMENTS

This book has become a reality because of the love and support of hundreds of people who have held the vision. I am especially indebted to Hal and Linda Kramer, Marion Weber, and Fred Berensmeir for their belief in this vision from its inception, for their love, and for their altruistic support throughout this long journey. And thank you to Brenda Rosen at Quest Books and Beth Hansen book designer for helping to make this book a truly luminous creation.

I am deeply grateful to Dio Neff, Leona Jamison, Carol Guion, Thomas Hurley III, Barbara McNeill, Liz Kalloch, Dick Adams, David Rosen, Georg Feuerstein, Ed and Amerinda Alpern, Dr. Elizabeth Behnke, Dr. Lee Sennela, Dr. Angeles Arrien, Dr. Michael Flanagin, Scott Hess, Collen Mauro, Nancy Stoddard, and Joshua Mailman for all the help and encouragement along the way. I thank my brother, Michael Russer, and my sisters, Jean, Joan Marie, and Marian for their loving support. I want to thank my friends who have added many blessings and much light to my life: Dr. Steve and Joanne Kairys, Dave and Jan Dunlop, Dana Boussard, Stan Reifel, Bob Shapiro, Shams Kairys, Nancy Swadesh, Dr. Sara Miseveth, Jenny Badger, Verity Dierauf.

My heartfelt appreciation to Dr. Willis Harman and Winston Franklin at The Institute of Noetic Sciences whose support helped to make this book a reality. The Institute was founded in 1973 by Edgar D. Mitchell, Apollo 14 astronaut, to engage in research, dialogue, and communication on issues concerning the human mind and consciousness and their role in the continuing evolution of humankind.

Deepest gratitude to the great sages and saints of all traditions, throughout all ages, for the gifts of illumination, wisdom, and love—they are a continual source of strength, blessing, and inspiration.

CONTENTS

CONTENTS

CONTENTS

PREFACE

Our deepest fear is not that we are inadequate. Our deepest fear is that we are powerful beyond measure. It is our light, not our darkness, that frightens us. We ask ourselves, who am I to be brilliant, gorgeous, talented, and fabulous? Actually, who are you not *to be? You are a child of God. . . . We were born to make manifest the glory of God within us . . . as we let our own light shine, we unconsciously give other people permission to do the same.*

Marianne Williamson, *A Return To Love*

Drawing the Light from Within was first published in 1990. Since that time I have traveled to many countries giving my transformative art workshops to thousands of people. My work has proved to me that everyone has an inner light of soul—a spark of the original creativity of the universe. This creativity is a soul gift, a birthright. When we cultivate it from a place of wisdom and love, we further evolution by expanding our consciousness to bring forth expressions of healing and harmony. The exercises in this book, which were developed and perfected in my workshops, can teach you to awaken your original creativity and to recreate your life as a work of art, which breathes into the world a spirit of unity, beauty, and peace.

Too often we regard our artistic endeavors as a hobby, something we do when there's no more important work to be done. However, the shared practice of sacred creativity can be a magical builder of community, whether in homes, businesses, or schools.

A powerful example of what can happen took place last summer when I was leading an art workshop at Hollyhock, a holistic educational center on Cortez Island, British Columbia. Famed Nigerian drummer Babatunde Olatunji was at Hollyhock at the same time, teaching his African drumming and chanting classes to an ethnically diverse group of teenagers and adults.

Over the years Babatunde and I had become friends, having taught workshops during the same weeks at Omega Institute in Rhinebeck, New York, and during various conferences across the United States. Baba, as he is affectionately called, had expressed

The unlimited Creative Principle within you is the source of all art and wisdom. When you want to create something important, sit quietly and meditate deeply upon it. You will be guided by the creative Spirit, but you should also exercise determination in accomplishing your objective. Awaken initiative, which is the creative faculty within you—a spark from the divine Creator. You must do something which will show that God's creative principle is active within you.

—Paramahansa Yogananda

respect for the work I do helping people to manifest their inner light. He suggested that we join forces to create a spiritual experience, bringing together his drumming group and my *Drawing the Light* group. I found the prospect exciting. Sound and light are both vibrations of energy, and using both drumming and drawing to activate the human imagination at inspired levels had enormous potential for demonstrating the potential of creative work as well as for healing the Earth.

Everyone at Hollyhock was invited, young children and mothers, fathers and sons, staff personnel, people taking nature courses, in addition to my drawing students and Baba's drumming students. In the end, a hundred people of all ages and from across the world joined together to pray, raise their voices in the sacred chants of Africa, and draw the inner light as luminous circular symbols.

We gathered in a large circle on the front lawn. Everyone was handed a small sheet of black paper with a circle drawn on it and a white drawing pencil. Students from my workshop spread through the crowd and quickly taught the participants to create a scale of light on the black paper as a representation of their inner light. Most of the people who participated had never had training in drawing. They were invited simply to hold a healing intention in their hearts and to ask during the ritual to have spirit reveal to them a perfect symbol that could both heal the Earth and represent to them their creative work in world.

Baba began the actual ritual by leading us in a blessing of the art materials. He then lead the chanting of a prayer, with the whole group repeating each part of the chant after him, accompanied by drummers. When the chanting was completed, there was silence, and in this sacred stillness, everyone including the children began to draw a radiant healing symbol. In about ten minutes, the drawings were complete. Everyone placed their luminous drawing on the ground in a circle, and the whole group did a walking meditation around them to the accompaniment of Baba's drumming. We held hands and stood in silence feeling our spiritual oneness, while marveling at the wonderful outpourings of our creativity. Though we each had held the same intention, each person had expressed the intention in a unique and powerful way.

This exercise brought together the collective inner light and the sacred sounds of consciousness to push a small group past the stultifying limits of cultural and religious prejudice, competition, isolating nationalism, and rational belief. It gave us the opportunity to reflect from the intuitive inner eye of contemplation the soul light that is in all of us. Each participant experienced the healing energies of our collective intentions vibrating as sacred chant and radiant soul drawings. Even very young children were calm, silent, and filled with awe. In this brief but profound moment, we shared in a beautiful flowering of our oneness with spirit and with our planet.

How can the experience of this group become universal? How can the powerful soul gifts of inner light, intuition, and imagination, through which we can jointly create a more wholesome world, become a new way of being on a large scale? The first step is awakening from the nightmare of seeing ourselves as limited beings. The more we hold to a diminished image of humanity, the more we become swallowed up and contracted by low self-esteem, hopelessness, and fear. When we believe ourselves to be without talent or power, we lack the energy we need to bring in new visions of our wholeness and of our connections with all life. Instead, we accept the dictates of a few who feed us images of destruction and project to us a sense of human hopelessness.

For more than twenty years, I have elected not to watch network television and its news because I found that the images and story lines were making me spiritually, psychologically, and physically ill. Many people do not realize that pictures and sounds have power to harm us. The vivid images the media generates become embedded in the brain as vibratory patterns of energy with tremendous power to influence us. A daily diet of poisonous pictures and negative words impacts negatively on the human psyche, affecting both the physical and chemical structure of the brain and the subtle energy systems of the body-mind. The media's daily dose of sensationalized brutality, sadistic violence, and greed has rendered us numb, or addicted to competition and dissension. Thousands of teenagers commit suicide today because they have no hope for the future—they foresee only violence and abuse. We have become a society turned to creative destruction—modeling the media's violent way of being in our arts, homes, businesses, and communities. We have collectively fallen into a self-defeating pattern of using our imaginative powers largely to perpetrate myopic vision, sexual and cultural prejudices, exclusionary social, business, political, and religious beliefs.

However, all is not lost. Embedded within our soul vision are the creative possibilities of our future. Our communities, the arts, music, scientific technologies, and businesses can become life-affirming, harmonious, beautiful, and healing institutions if we are willing to awaken to inspired states of imagination, intuition, and creativity. These gifts are the means through which we manifest our individual spark of Divine Light. Practicing them with wisdom, love, and compassion, we can contribute to a spiritual renaissance, in which our human creations reflect the true Light of divinity and through which we can re-make our world.

We are each soul stars, born to manifest our part of a divine constellation of Light. If we do not allow this Light to shine, we create from the darkness of fear. As different as stars, each human soul has unique gifts that have been given to it to shine forth. We inhabit an intelligent universe that continues to manifest an infinite variety of forms. As a participant in the field of this endlessly generating world, the human imagination will always yield an infinite diversity of expressions—artistic, scientific, and religious.

Each of us is like a gleaming facet on the diamond, an aspect of the sacred wholeness of the Divine Light. When we express our portion of this Light from a place of love, we mirror the one radiant Self out of which we are born. Never was there a better time to bring forth new images shining with the soul's splendor.

Judith Cornell, 1997

FOREWORD

We have not yet assimilated this century's most far-reaching discovery, namely that energy, or light, is the principle underlying all manifestation. In other words, we have not yet grasped that we— our bodies and our minds—are *light.*

In this book, Judith Cornell applies Einstein's epoch-making formula $E = mc^2$ to artistic creativity. She has developed an approach to painting and drawing that is an important breakthrough.

Drawing from the tradition of sacred art, which has long known of the mystery of light (as the matrix of all existence) and of our cocreativity in the world process, Dr. Cornell has formulated principles and techniques that help awaken and express the artist in us. Her remarkable work with ordinary people from all walks of life demonstrates the immense effectiveness of her approach.

It is the author's philosophy that art, like light, is an inalienable part of human nature. Her unique teaching method is meant to put us in touch with that deeper aspect of our being. To live in the light, to live in resonance with that incommensurable dimension of energy that is our very source, we must become artists. Conversely, if we wish to create authentic art, we must be in touch with the living reality of the radiant energy that is the "stuff" of our body-minds and the world.

Judith Cornell shows that in order to manifest and enjoy our creative potential as makers of art, that is, as cocreators of the universe, we must go beyond our presumed limitations and envision a different, more comprehensive reality. True art is always yoga, or spiritual practice: a dynamic contemplation of the mystery in which we and everything else arise. And true human life is art.

Her approach, which entails visualizations modeled on Indian Tantric art, is an effective way of tapping the imaginative power that our left-brained civilization is neglecting and even suppressing to all our detriment. However, this book is not merely another variation on the theme of exploiting the right brain to outwit the left cerebral hemisphere. Dr. Cornell's interest is in the *whole* person—both sides of the brain as well as the rest of the body-mind, which contains far greater mysteries than the lateralization of the human cortex.

Judith Cornell's inspired method of teaching art helps us to unblock neurotic obstructions and it also allows the artistic process to come alive as part of our personal growth toward transparency. So long as we do not truly understand ourselves, we remain opaque, blocking out the primordial light. Only through deep self-knowledge do we gain the kind of transparency that renders us pervious to the light within us. Then we also drop the solid walls by which we ordinarily defend ourselves against the light and the beauty in others. What nobler task could there be for art? What greater challenge and responsibility could there be for the person—you and me?

I wish to thank Judith Cornell for sharing her bright vision of art and life with us in her many years of teaching and now in this book.

—GEORG FEUERSTEIN, M. LIT.
Author, *Structures of Consciousness,*
Yoga: The Technology of Ecstasy, and
Introduction to the Bhagavad-Gita

INTRODUCTION: BEFORE YOU BEGIN THIS BOOK

All great art is a bridge to the beyond. It is an urging of man's soul to a higher, better world of being—a world that we are given the power and command to create on earth.[1]

—RUTH HARWOOD, *Cosmic Art*

Is creativity a learnable skill? Does everyone possess the ability to perform extraordinary feats that we commonly ascribe to only a few? Can expanded states of consciousness and creativity be reached without the aid of drugs or years of intensive training? Can problem-solving processes in drawing and painting provide insights into solving the challenges we face as human beings living together on this earth? These are some of the questions I addressed in developing my teaching method and writing this book. In every instance, the answer is emphatically *yes*. The exercises in this book reveal a powerful way of thinking and observing that I believe is necessary now more than ever in the push and pull of daily life.

HOW TO USE THIS BOOK

This book is meant for you and anyone wishing to develop creativity—laypersons, teachers, philosophers, scientists, psychologists, and designers, as well as visual artists. "Where do I begin in this book?" you might ask. I would suggest at first that you enjoy browsing through the pictures in the book. It will give you a glimpse of the unlimited potential, beauty, and genius present within every human being. The artwork in this book was not created by talented, trained artists but by average citizens from all over the world. These people—men and women of all ages, walks of life, and cultural backgrounds—had little or no training in art when they enrolled in my beginning drawing and design classes at City College of San Francisco, California. Within a four-month period, they came to execute these outstanding works of vision and inspiration.

As you read the students' quotes, you will find that they initially believed that they had little artistic ability. Like most people, they had no understanding of their own potent creativity until they stepped past their fears and, using the exercises in these chapters, learned to take creative risks. These exercises were specifically designed to attune people to their intuitive power and to develop what I call our inner light. The idea that inner light is real and accessible to all of us is fundamental to the method presented in this book.

INNER LIGHT:
A SPIRITUAL EXPRESSION IN ART

From ancient times, inner light has been an experiential phenomena of mystics and sages as well as a central theme in the sacred literature and art of most religious traditions. Inner light is *real*, more real than many phenomena we accept as reality. As Dr. Ralph Metzner points out in his book *Opening to Inner Light*:

> Medieval philosophers made a distinction between three kinds of light and three kinds of eyes . . . we have *eyes of flesh*, which see with exterior light . . . the physical world of sense objects and matter. Next, we have an *eye of reason*, which sees the interior light, the truths of reason, mind, and knowledge. Last, we have an *eye of contemplation*, which sees with higher or transcendent light the ultimate reality of oneness, the ground of Being. (italics added)[2]

Through the guided visualization exercises and practical skill-building projects in this book, you will be shown how to "see" with "the eye of contemplation" and use your own inner light to create beautiful works of art. The projects are designed specifically to help you surmount the fear and self-judgments that stifle creative power.

KEYS TO AWAKEN THE ARTIST WITHIN YOU

Each chapter leads you step by step into the wisdom that resides within you. In the process, you will learn to use a wide range of art materials. The projects are designed to give you both skills and sensitivity for attaining that unique level of awareness usually attributed to the rare genius. Throughout the chapters you'll find special "keys" to awaken the artist within you. The keys, which uncover important truths common to all of us, are integrated into the art methods and combined with recent scientific insights.

PAINTING AND DRAWING WITH LIGHT

The book includes both painting and drawing projects. You can choose to begin in either area. If you like painting (or think you might), begin with chapter 1. If you feel more comfortable with drawing, begin with chapter 3.

PAINTING WITH LIGHT

Chapters 1 and 2 show how to use simple water-based paints creatively. If you have always wanted to learn about color and paint mixing, these chapters will give you a joyful experience of color and light. You will learn the difference between seeing with the eye of reason and seeing and creating with your inner light. You also will learn to develop the powers of your imagination and intuition.

DRAWING WITH LIGHT

Chapters 3 through 6 reveal easy ways to achieve dramatic results using various drawing pencils and paper. Each chapter will deepen your understanding of the difference between drawing your inner light and drawing the exterior light of the phenomenal world. You will learn how to see with the eye of contemplation when you work on projects.

HOW MY METHOD OF INTEGRAL ART EVOLVED

Integral means whole. Integral Art is a method of creating from a sense of unity, love, and joy by learning to see with all of our "eyes." My pioneering work of creating this new model of art

KEYS

- Expanding consciousness
- Honoring the unity of all life
- Releasing fear
- Opening your heart to unconditional love
- Developing your intuitive power
- Trusting the wisdom within you
- Accessing inspired states of imagination
- Deciding not to compete
- Visualizing your inner light
- Utilizing inspirational music or sacred sound
- Manifesting your inner light through your art

education that incorporates both spiritual and scientific elements began in the late 1970s as a result of an intense spiritual/physical transformation. At the time, I was searching for a universal principle to express in my own artwork—one that would convey the deepest possible truth about all aspects of life. I asked myself, "What is the underlying essence of all reality?" The answer came to me quickly—*light!*

ILLUMINATION

What I envisioned at that moment appeared to me to be a glimpse of human evolution—a profoundly moving picture in my brain of the unfolding divine human ability to coparticipate in the creation of the phenomenal world by using and directing light. I perceived light as both a physical energy defined by the electromagnetic spectrum *and* as the spiritual energy often experienced by meditators as inner light of consciousness. For me, physical and spiritual light were *integrated* as one.

Very early in my professional development, long before my intuitive insight, I concluded that art—that is, the talent to create—was not limited to a few chosen people but inherent in all humankind. With great certainty, I saw that all people are artists in that they *actively create their lives each day,* whether they are creating bridges, making ceramics, inventing new electronics, constructing business ventures, solving problems, rearing children, creating some new gastronomic treat, or redecorating a home. This expanded definition of *artist* marked me as a rebel.

As a result of the illuminative experience, I realized the power of my own mind to distort and fragment my experience of life. As an artist I discovered that when my consciousness was based on fear, I felt fragmented in mind, body, and spirit and produced disjointed, dissonant imagery in art. This realization was my first that *the mind has the power to alter both internal and external reality,* depending on how it is focused.

When the mind is focused on inner light, in a state of love, the eye of contemplation pierces the illusions of the outer world and sees the underlying unity of all life. But if the mind is experiencing fear, and sees with only the physical eyes or with the eye of reason, then the mind becomes judgmental and perceives the world as fragmented, hostile, and separate from the self.

LIGHT AS A KEY

I reasoned that if my intuitive insight about light had occurred for me, then each individual, like myself, would also have innate knowledge about spiritual and physical light. Could I help students unlock this inner knowledge? I found that one key to unlocking this knowledge was for students to *visualize* their inner light. Special guided visualizations for seeing inner light became an integral part of my method. They are shared in this book.

Since my students have included people of all ages, I was able to observe what happens to the creativity of people as they mature. The children had great imaginations and enthusiasm for creative expression. But I noticed that as they grew up, people felt more and more fear about expressing themselves creatively. That fear created a state of paralysis, preventing them from developing their fullest power of creativity. Experiencing this state myself and seeing it happen so predictably in other people was another major step in the evolution of my teaching method. I had to find a way to guide students past their fear.

UNCONDITIONAL LOVE
AND
NONCOMPETITIVENESS AS KEYS

Great spiritual masters such as Christ, Buddha, Krishna, Mother Theresa, Alice Bailey, Sri Aurobindo, Mahatma Gandhi, and Yogananda, to name but a few, spoke of the great power of unconditional love. Unconditional love is a state of nonjudgment and respect for the divinity of the human family. I learned that the secret for helping students past their fear was to give them unconditional love and to help them open their hearts to love. I practiced holding the intention of love in my mind during my classes, and saw that it created a nonthreatening atmosphere conducive to helping people reach expanded states of creativity. Unconditional love and nonjudgment support the unlimited creative development for the highest good of the individual.

ART AS A SACRED PRACTICE

As my thinking and research took me down many paths, old and new, I became familiar with a number of spiritual traditions in which art is considered a sacred practice. In particular, I found similarities for the methods I was developing in the ancient Hindu tradition and practice of Tantric art. *Tantra* comes from the Sanskrit word *tan,* to expand consciousness.

MUSIC AND SOUND AS A KEY

Tantra is a yogic practice based on contemplation and meditation that emphasizes sacred sounds (mantras) and the visualization of inner light with the purpose of understanding the hidden meaning of reality. The central doctrine of Indian Tantra is that every thought originates in sound, and that the sound produces a geometric construct that manifests itself into a form of light. Through this sacred practice, the artist acquires the power to remake the vision of himself or herself and—through art—of the world. Practicing art in this way leads the yogi toward truth and the realization of spiritual powers. Borrowing from this concept of sacred sound, I incorporated the use of inspiring music in the classroom to create an atmosphere conducive to expanded states of consciousness.

In the Tantric tradition, *visualization* was considered a supreme way to access knowledge. It was through visualization and contemplation—*not* through observation of tangible objects—that one gained knowledge of the nature of reality. Through the spiritual practice of art, the yogi came to realize that the individual and the universe were all one and that what exists in the universe also exists in the individual.[3]

NEW PHYSICS AND SACRED ART

When enrolled in a joint doctoral program focusing on art and philosophy, I began to do some serious reading in *new physics.* In the research of these brilliant scientists and thinkers, I found a confirmation of the Tantric insights—a realization that the individual and the universe are all one—that "both observer and observed are merging and interpenetrating aspects of one whole reality."[4] Research in subatomic physics is yielding a new view of reality. The material world is made of atoms and electromagnetic energies (light in its broadest definition). It appears solid and stationary. In actual fact, however, this solidity is illusionary. Physicist Fritjof Capra describes this new view of matter:

> The energy patterns of the subatomic world form stable atomic and molecular structures that build up matter and give it its macroscopic solid appearance, thus making us believe it is made of some material substance . . . Atoms consist of particles and these particles are not made of any material stuff. When we observe them we never see any substance; what we observe are dynamic patterns continually changing into one another—a continuous dance of energy.[5]

Because of this research, we have also discovered our ability to unleash energies of the atom and other forms of electromagnetic energies. This discovery has lead to a new image of our "real" creative power to change all aspects of life on our planet.

I used visualization to integrate this new view of matter and new image of human potential into my teaching. The idea is to visualize the very materials used to make art—the paints, paper, brushes, and so on—as being composed of pulsating light and energy. This visualization helps us to comprehend physical reality not as separate parts and pieces but as a living web of dancing energies in which we as human beings powerfully participate.

BRAIN RESEARCH AND ANCIENT INSIGHTS

Ancient wisdom teachings now are also supported by the latest model of human potential emerging from contemporary brain research, which shows that our schools and society have discriminated against the part of our brain that regulates many of our creative functions—those of intuition, imagination, visualization, and spatial perception. Nobel prize winner Robert Sperry's work supports the necessity to include consciousness as a real energy of creative choice:

One of the more important things to come out of brain research in recent years is a modified concept of the nature of the conscious mind and its relation to brain mechanism . . . Instead of renouncing or ignoring consciousness, the new interpretation gives full recognition to inner conscious awareness as an important high-level directive force or property in the brain mechanism.[6]

This new scientific perspective gives much needed support to children and adults who are so often discouraged from using the mind's powers of imagination and intuition. Many of my students have been warned since childhood against using their imaginations or trusting their hunches—nonrational promptings of their intuition.

AN INTEGRAL APPROACH TO ART IS NOT DOGMATIC

I have found this integral approach to be a powerful tool in unlocking a person's ability to manifest his or her unique sense of beauty and order. However, it is not meant as the last word or for use in a dogmatic way. You need not even understand the integral approach or believe in its truths in order to use it and benefit from it. But if you take up this book and follow the exercises, your particular life experiences and inner light will make this approach your own. In addition, you will prove for yourself that you can make art that is more beautiful than you believed was possible—pictures luminescent with the light of your own truth and vision.

NOTES

1. Raymond F. Piper and Lila K. Piper, Ingo Swann, ed., *Cosmic Art* (New York: Hawthorn Books, 1975), 132.
2. Ralph Metzner, *Opening to Inner Light* (Los Angeles: Jeremy P. Tarcher, Inc., 1986), 76.
3. Ajit Mookerjee, *Tantric Art* (New Delhi: Ravi Kumar Publisher, 1983), 18–19.
4. David Bohm, *Wholeness and the Implicate Order* (London: Routlege, Chatman and Paul, 1980), 9.
5. Fritjof Capra, *Ancient Wisdom & Modern Science* (Albany, New York: State University of New York Press, 1984), 137. Reprinted with permission.
6. Roger Sperry, *Science & Moral Priority* (New York: Columbia University Press, 1983), 59.

What is now proved was once only imagined.

—William Blake

Imagination is more important than knowledge.

—Albert Einstein

Every human being has some spark of power by which he can create something that has not been created before.

—Paramahansa Yogananda

CHAPTER 1

Painting with Light

*In Great Eternity every particular Form gives forth or Emanates Its own peculiar
Light, and the Form is the Divine Vision And the Light is his Garment. This is the
Jerusalem in every man.*

—William Blake[1]

WILLIAM BLAKE, the nineteenth-century visionary poet and artist, contended that true freedom, liberty, and equality were based on the expression by each individual of his or her own "peculiar Light." Blake called it the divine light or "Jerusalem in every man." It is by expressing this internal radiance and "divine vision" that a person can become a true artist and original genius. This book will help you discover the "peculiar Light" within yourself and the materials with which you work. The exercises in this chapter will focus on the traditional gray scale—the gradations of gray that take us from white to black. You will explore the "peculiar Light" of the gray scale using water-soluble paints—and, without knowing you, based on my classroom experience, I can guarantee you dramatic results.

My students, all beginning art students, achieved the exciting work you see in this chapter using ordinary black-and-white opaque water-soluble paints. These pictures were born through the two projects you will work on later in the chapter:

- Creating a gray scale from black-and-white paints
- Painting a design while envisioning black-and-white paint not simply as pigment but—quite literally—as light and energy

If you look at the student work in this chapter, you will see not only a diversity of designs but many unique expressions of light and luminescence. This work is no small feat for beginners who have had virtually no training or color-mixing experience. Through the ages, artists painting either sacred or secular subject matter have striven hard to achieve subtle effects of light and luminescence in their work. How is it possible that untrained students can achieve so much in their very first color-mixing experience?

FREEING YOUR VISION BY CHANGING CONSCIOUSNESS

The key is to replace our traditional concept of *gray* with the perception of gray as *light* and *energy*. Quite simply, my students achieved these wonderful effects with black-and-white paints *by changing the focus of their minds*. Normally, artists think of gray as any of a series of gradations from black to white produced by mixing black-and-white paint together. In art, gray is thought of as having no pure color or hue. In this context, if a person focuses the mind on the word *gray,* the brain responds with the traditional image of gray as most people have been taught to perceive it. Words such as *dull, dark, dismal,* and *gloomy* come to our minds.

The true nature of black-and-white pigments, however, is not gray at all. Black and white are *pure energy* composed of atoms and photons of light. Black pigments *absorb* all visible light rays and white pigments *reflect* all visible light rays. Black-and-white pigments together, then, both reflect and absorb all colors of visible light. When you learn in this chapter to *focus on your inner light* and expand your consciousness in working with black-and-white pigments by perceiving these ordinary pigments as *light and atomic realities,* you will be able to produce results as inspiring and luminescent as the examples given here.

LOSING THE FEAR THAT BINDS

You may have been drawn to this book because of its beautiful inspirational images and a sense that inside you there is an artist waiting to be born. Or perhaps you have feared that there is no creative talent inside you, yet you know deep down that something is missing in your life. You may believe that you could not possibly achieve such splendor as the pictures in this chapter achieve. Such fears, doubts, and inner longings are not unusual, and you are not alone in your thoughts. Many before you have felt the same way. For this reason I have included, along with the exercises that follow, stories of how my students overcame their fears and unlocked the artist within. As you read these stories and study the pictures, the idea of gray as a shimmering scale of light will gradually take hold in your mind, replacing the traditional sense of gray as lifeless— and lightless—and you will be ready to build your own scale of light. These students' stories also give you a more fundamental gift: the reassurance that art is the gateway for everyone—not just trained artists—to a spiritual participation in the universe, and that whatever brought you to the study of art was an impulse toward the deepening of your experience of life itself.

The painting in figure 1-1 was done by Stan, a salesman with no previous art training. On his first attempt at visualizing black and white as energy, Stan produced an adequate design, but it was static and gray and conveyed no sense of light. Here it serves as a good example of the use of gray as it is *traditionally* understood. The picture falls short of the assignment's objective, which is to produce a design using the *full value scale* of light in a number of different ways. In music, if one uses only a single note on the scale, the result is not music. In art, if one uses only a single gradation of paint, the result is not light. I explained that the assignment was to use a *full* scale of at least nine gradations of light in logical order, going from pure black (absorbing light) to pure white (reflecting light). Once the concept of a scale of light took hold in Stan's mind, he did another design (figure 1-2) that was highly successful in displaying the dynamics of light and luminescence.

Figure 1-1

Figure 1-2

If you study this design you will notice that it is a simple symmetrical composition using diamond and triangle shapes. A basic design such as this might not entice the viewer to look at it twice. But Stan went beyond the ordinary and made this symmetrical design dynamic by using the full scale of light in each of the shapes. For Stan to accomplish this exciting sense of luminescence involved more than just the analytical use of the full scale. Stan had to involve his whole being in the creative process: his mind, imagination, intuition, and his inner light.

By using gradation in a design to show the movement of light you can cause the eye to move. You can make things appear near and far. I feel that a whole new awareness is coming to me as I learn the basics.

—Stan

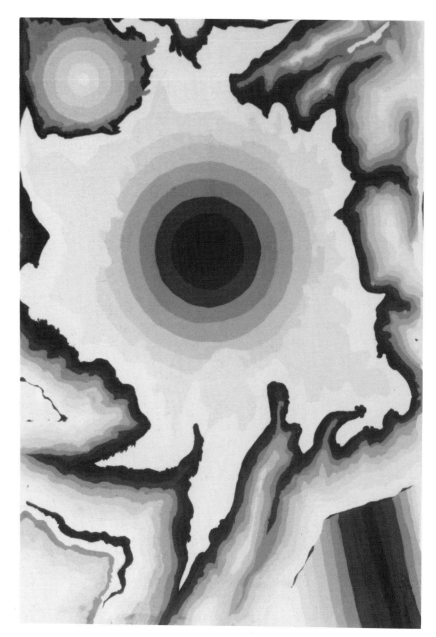

Figure 1-3

I learned that the design comes from within. The light must illuminate your consciousness. I was worried that I didn't have the ability to do this assignment. The reality is that art/design is within you. That anything I want is within myself. Fear is always the problem, but when overcome it ceases to be.

—STEVEN

Figure 1-4

I want to draw and I want to paint and I know I can do it and more . . . I need to. There is nothing in my way except fear and insecurity, and those seem very small now.

—LILLI

At nineteen, Lilli had no art training. She had to overcome many fears to take this design class. In this project she experienced a major breakthrough to an expanded state of creativity.

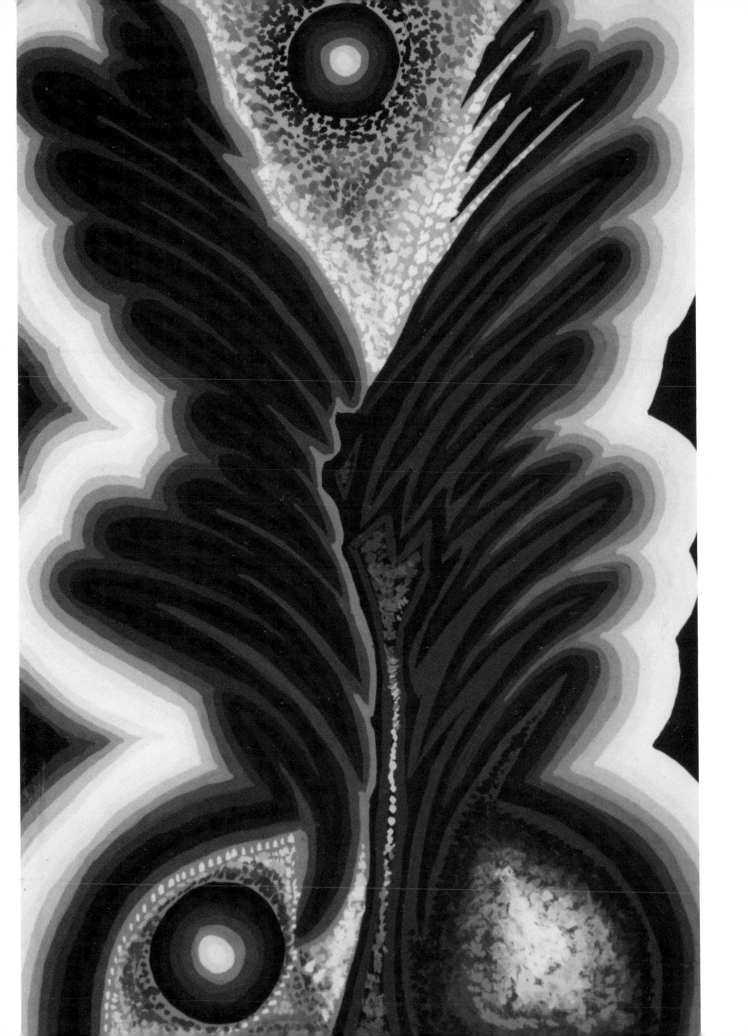

When Steven took my design class he was in his twenties and working full time as a word processor (see figure 1-3). Like most of the students in my evening classes, he was looking for more meaning and purpose in life. Intuitively he turned to art for spiritual nourishment, but he had been advised by others to drop art and pursue a business degree. He had also been told that he'd never get into an art school because he hadn't started making art as a child. This misconception is common and reflects limiting and conservative views generally held regarding human creative potential. Even worse, it reflects the view that the practice of art is inessential to human development. I asked Steve to write his reason for taking this class, and his response follows:

I want to have a career that is art-centered because I love art. I love colors, forms, and substances that I can mold and form into beautiful shapes or contours. I'm tired of conforming and listening to people tell me how to run my life. I won't listen anymore. I am taking this class so that I can expand into a space far away from a technological society—away from computers, away from the material universe into more of the spiritual universe. Art is expressive . . . of the soul's desire.

Marshall, another design student, explained the either/or dilemma—success or art—that dominates our ambition-fueled society:

The things that have inhibited [my] creativity are primarily schooling (in particular), society (in general), and, during my adult life, the expectations of the professional world.

In high school, instructors and counselors always stressed the practical, "serious," academic classes. I remember one occasion quite distinctly: I asked my counselor what he thought of my taking an art class in the next semester. He gave me an incredulous look and replied, "Well, if that's what you think you really want to do."

In the professional world, most managers and those who can help one advance in a career don't give much credence to classes in the evening. It comes down to the age-old debate: Study something structured and possibly help yourself jobwise or take an art class and watch management collectively shake their heads.

Figure 1-5. Robert incorporated a softly pulsing scale of luminescence coming into the center of the design. Unlike the other students whose work appears in this chapter, he used only one major light scale to achieve the effect of light, but the way he used it—as a central point of interest—gives mystery to the compelling glow that draws the viewer's attention inward.

Marshall ignored the discouragement he received, but Robert, like a number of students I have had, internalized it, and thus struggled with the fear of success and commitment to his artistic impulses. He expressed how fear can stand between us and literally anything we wish to do:

> I was always afraid to devote myself to anything. I always considered that giving 100 percent of myself to any endeavor was stupid, a waste of time. In the end we all die and our great works are reduced to ashes. Time is wasted if it is spent on future hopes. Only the moment counts.

Not surprisingly, Robert found himself struggling with the meaning and purpose of life. To remain creative he had to make an active commitment to give birth to the art within. His solution to the design problem (figure 1-5) shows a great deal of sensitivity and artistic talent. By refusing to give in to his fears and by making a committed effort, he achieved a beautiful design, unique in its use of the light scale.

Figure 1-6

I was afraid I wouldn't be able to create a design, but when I let my hand go it created a design I approved of. What amazes me is that I'm doing anything at all. I was never able to do anything like this before, so I really respect the "doing" of it. The visualization technique is dynamic. And I'm willing to learn more about what I can do.

—MELISSA

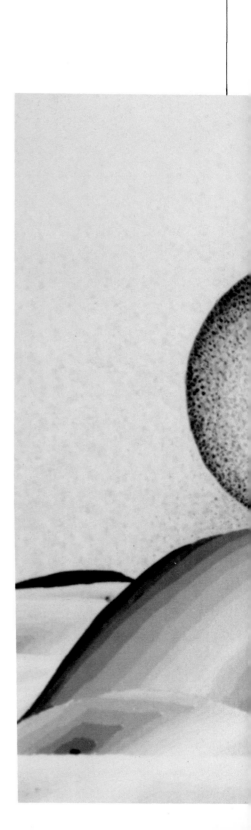

Figure 1-7. Robert had some design background before he took my class. His originality in expressing light and design is highly sophisticated. He achieved a soft luminescent effect by starting at the middle of the scale and proceeding to white. In part of his design he achieves the full scale of light by using dots of color—a technique not unlike one used by the Impressionist painters. I did not teach soft luminescence or the use of dots in the class; Robert came to this knowledge intuitively.

One student, Martha, brought with her not discouragement or alienation but a wealth of stimulating connections and insights from the outside world. She was a professional molecular biologist who at age thirty took my class to develop her creative talents. Though talented and happy in her work, she came to me with doubts about her creative potential in the visual arts. "As a child I wasn't encouraged to be myself," she told me. "I was not given much praise, and as a result I was very insecure and had many self-doubts. I suffer from a tendency to compare myself with the others in class. Once I relax I bet I'll turn into Michelangelo!" Her reference was a joke, but the scintillating blend of artistic and scientific vision in her work is related to the same masterful blending that marked Michelangelo's genius (figure 1-8).

Figure 1-8. Martha's design reflects her involvement in genetic research. The image she created using various imaginative and repetitive scales of light is reminiscent of the shape of a DNA molecule. In the field of science, Martha is actually very involved in the creative process. She changes the bioelectromagnetic structure of DNA to create new life forms. Blending her knowledge and creativity from science and the visual arts, she captures on paper the beauty, intricacy, and energy of life at the microscopic level.

As is clear from the remarks that accompany the pictures in this chapter (see particularly figure 1-10), people experience a great sense of accomplishment when they complete this project. They discover that there is something magical and compelling about the radiance of light, especially light that they themselves have released using ordinary paint pigments. It is important to mention that the environment these students worked in was one of noncompetitiveness and cooperative learning. Only in such a context can people be free of their accumulated fears and preconceived notions about art.

Figure 1-9

Figure 1-10

June had been out of school for more than thirty years. Her fear was that she would not be able to keep up with the rest of the students. She overcame her fear by involving herself enthusiastically in the creative process. June's painting reflects her spontaneity, joyousness, love, and ability to express her own inner light.

I am so surprised at the beautiful light formations that the gradation system brings forth. I am truly enjoying the creative juices that flow when it's time to put it on paper.

—Jᴜɴᴇ

My fear was that I would participate only mechanically, that I would not understand or create the feeling of light. How excited I became as I slowly put the colors together and saw the shapes begin to move and glow! I imagined floating in a swirling universe, watching black holes, worlds turn. . . . And before me I saw my vision begin to happen. I was very pleased at my accomplishment. I learned that it is possible to create "magic" in a methodical way— step by step, gradation by gradation. Magic is not the gift for genius use only.

—LEANNE

Figure 1-11

CREATING AN INSPIRING ENVIRONMENT WITH MUSIC

One important key to this safe and stress-free ambience is *music,* classical and inspirational—the particular kind of music known to be conducive to the meditative state. I play it in the classroom when students are working on their assignments. I urge you to play such music while working on all projects in this book. See the Appendix for a list of suggestions and resources.

Turn now to the gray-scale problem that allowed these people to contribute so richly to the beauty, radiance, and knowledge of light.

Figure 1-12

PART 1: THE GRAY SCALE AS A SCALE OF LIGHT

The gray scale is a series of gradations from black to white. Traditionally, it is the backbone of the color systems. In color work it is used to determine the *value range* or *scale of differences* between dark and light colors.

PROJECT: CREATING A SCALE OF LIGHT

This project will teach you how to mix opaque black-and-white paints to create the gray scale shown in figure 1-13. You will use this scale as a reference for doing the project in part 2, where you will paint a design while envisioning white and black paint as light and energy. Later, in chapter 2, you will use your gray scale as a basic tool in mixing and using colored paints. Further, this scale of light will be a reference for the projects you will do in chapters 5 and 6, although in these chapters you will be using an entirely different art medium—pencil. Clearly, then, your gray scale will be a very important tool as you progress through the book. It will also introduce you to the most basic tenet of this method—that *to manipulate pigments means literally to handle light itself.* By the end of this chapter you literally will be painting with light.

Figure 1-13. Scale of light. The traditional gray scale illustrated here gives the sense that gray is dynamic: filled with light and energy. To bring this idea into the realm of our consciousness, we will call this value scale a scale of light.

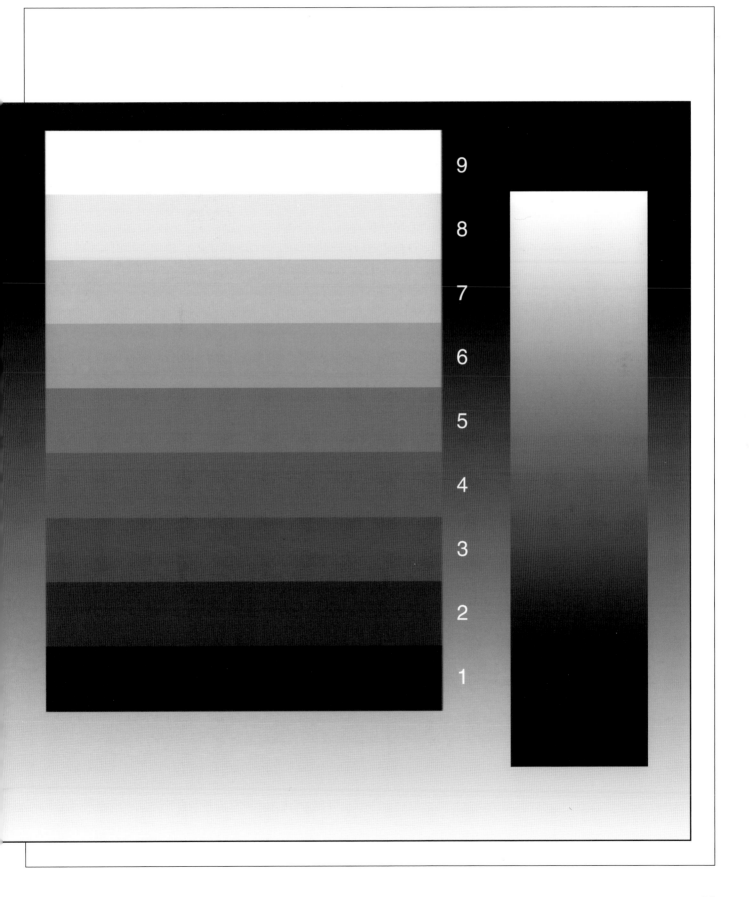

MATERIALS

- 14-by-17-inch white drawing pad (any kind will do)
- 14-by-17-inch Bristol board pad—smooth texture, medium weight
- Regular pencil
- Ruler
- Scissors
- Water container
- High-quality # 6 sable watercolor brush with a pointed tip
- Small sable # 1 detail brush
- Plastic mixing tray that can hold twelve or more mixed pigments
- Rubber cement (you can use another kind of glue, but rubber cement is easy to use and cleans up nicely)
- Paper towels
- Small one-half-inch-wide roll of masking tape or magic removable tape
- One sheet of graphite-colored transfer paper
- High-quality brand of poster paint or designer gouache, white and jet black (In the project you will use more white paint than black, so get a half pint of white and a small container of black. A couple of high-quality brands are Liquitex Tempra and Winsor Newton designer gouaches.)
- Records and tapes of inspirational music (see Appendix)
- Special guided visualization tapes for this chapter and others (optional; see Appendix)

Figure 1-14. Illustration of a 9-by-5-inch format.

PROCEDURES

1. On a sheet of drawing paper, measure out a 9-by-5-inch rectangle. Divide that rectangle into 1-inch squares. Put the rectangle aside for a moment. You'll use only one side of the rectangle for this project; you'll use the other squares in the next chapter when you work on color (see figure 1-14).

2. Take out a sheet of white Bristol board paper, your paints, # 6 watercolor brush, water container, and mixing tray. Fill one of the depressions in your mixing tray with white paint and another one with black paint. If the depressions are large, you need not fill them up all the way.

3. Check to see that your paint has the texture of smooth cream. If it is stiff, add a little water and mix it until it takes on a creamy smoothness. Now you are ready to begin.

4. On your sheet of Bristol board, paint a band of pure white, wide enough so that you will eventually be able to cut out a 1-inch square. Next, take a small amount of black on the tip of your brush and put it into the white. *Be sure to mix it well with the white. Pretend you are stirring a pot of soup.* You will not notice much of a color change, but paint this mixture next to the white on the Bristol board paper.

5. Pick up some more black paint on your brush and again mix it into the white paint. *A useful hint for color mixing: Always add the darker color to the lighter color.* Each time you mix more black into the white, paint a band of that mixture onto the paper. Repeat this procedure until you have a broad range of values, colors that go all the way from white to black.

6. Toward the end of your mixing, you will find that there is very little white paint left and that it is almost totally absorbed by the black. At the end, paint a band of pure black.

7. While you are waiting for the paint to dry, take a piece of Bristol board paper 3 by 3 inches and measure a 1-inch square in the center. Using scissors, cut out the 1-inch square, which will be your template or pattern for tracing square shapes on top of your painted bands (see figure 1-15).

8. Using a regular pencil and the template you just made, trace a square on the band of black paint and on the band of white paint. Cut out the squares. Glue the white square on the top left-hand side of your 9-by-12-inch rectangle, and glue the black square at the bottom left side.

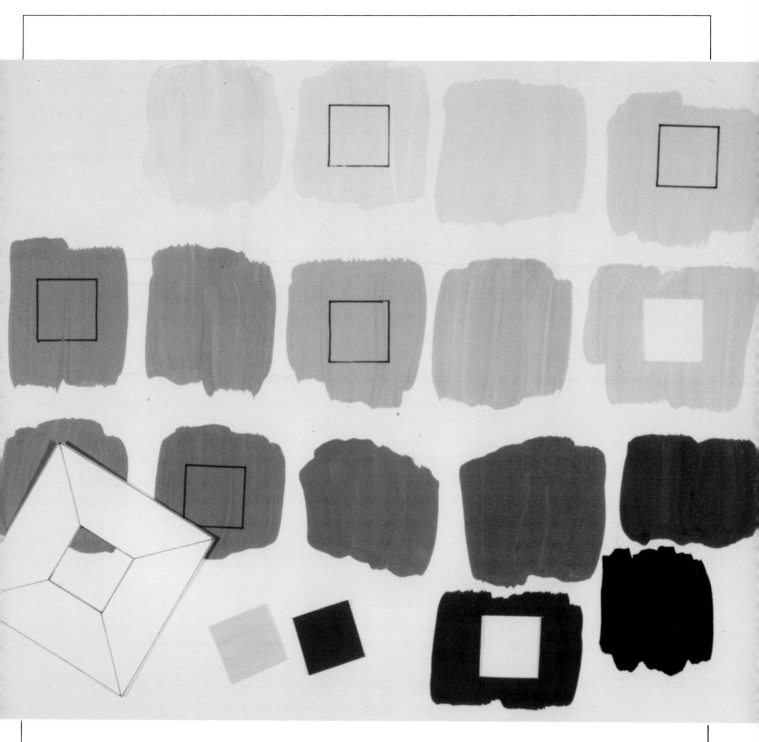

Figure 1-15. *After painting your scale of light, cut one-inch squares from your painted strips. These square paint strips will then be glued down on your 9-by-15-inch format in logical order (see figure 1-16).*

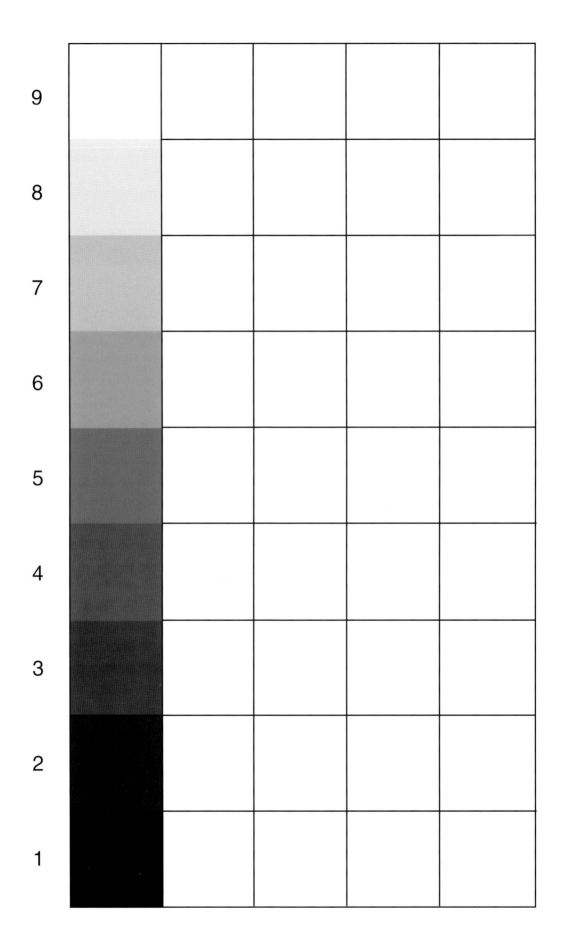

9. Go back to your paint samples and choose seven variations that proceed from light gray to the darkest charcoal gray. Trace a 1-inch square on each. Cut out the squares. Arrange these squares vertically on the rectangle, starting with the lightest gray under the white and proceeding to the darkest charcoal next to the black. The idea is to develop a harmonious visual sequence.

- Beware of putting grays that are too similar in color next to each other.
- Before gluing down the squares you have cut out, check to see that there is a logical progression from white to black. If there is not, go back to your paint samples and cut out other grays.
- Use the scale in this book as a visual guide.

CREATING LIGHT WITH THE COMPUTER

Over the years many people have asked me about the programs I use to create radiant images of light using the computer. The exercises in chapters 1 and 2 are particularly suited for the computer. In the Afterword (p. 199) I suggest the basic equipment and programs you will need.

There are several good drawing programs that make it quite easy to create luminous gradient scales of light. However, it is a mistake to think that if you have expensive computer equipment and a high-powered professional graphics program you will be able to create great art. First you need a grounding in good basic design. Then, you must understand the principles of inner and outer light and use this understanding to access inspired states of creativity. Whether you use the computer or paints as a medium of expression, you can gain better results and deeper knowledge by practicing the inner light meditation before you do the exercises.

Figure 1-16. Creating your own scale of light. This illustration shows you the proper place of your painted scale of light on the 9-by-5-inch format. Before you glue down the scale, check to see that you have a smooth series of gradations going from white to black.

TRADING GRAY FOR LIGHT

Traditionally, black and white pigments mixed together have been described as shades of gray. But for the purposes of the projects in this chapter—and for the rest of the book and for the rest of your life!—we need to eliminate the word *gray* from our vocabulary altogether. From this point on, then, we will think of white and black paint as purely light and energy. Why? *Because whatever the mind focuses on will determine the results in art.* Using new words gives the brain a new image with which to work. In this project, you want to ask the mind to imagine paints in terms of electromagnetic energies and to focus attention on your own inner light. Before you begin work on the projects in part 2, put on some music that uplifts you spiritually and makes you feel happy, relaxed, and motivated.

Trading Gray for Light
A VISUALIZATION

To focus your mind, consciously imagine the solar energies of the universe. Picture glowing atoms forming into molecules, which then grow into various shapes and forms. Then hold your paint containers in your hand, and with your eyes closed imagine that these materials are but a collection of atoms glowing with light and energy.

At first such visualizations will require your conscious effort, as with the learning of any new skill. But soon you will find that you are truly painting with light, and your pictures will be charged with luminescence. If you do not make the effort to begin imagining in these terms, your mind will hold on to the word *gray* and your work will reflect the tone of gray rather than exciting gradations of light. Here are a number of key points to help you in your visualizations:

- Visualize the paints as being electromagnetic energy.
- Imagine black paint to be black energy holes in the cosmos absorbing light. As with black holes, all energy is absorbed so that no light can be emitted.
- Imagine the white paint to be reflecting light and energy. White light reflects rather than absorbs.
- Imagine that the paints are black light and white light that produce a scale of light when they are combined.
- Focus your mind on the scale you made and visualize it as a *musical scale of light*. To play music, you need more than one note. And to use light and energy dynamically (as in part 2 of this project), you will need to use the full light scale in a number of creative ways.

PART 2: WHITE AND BLACK AS LIGHT AND ENERGY

PROJECT 1: CREATING A LINE DESIGN FOR YOUR PAINTING

MATERIALS

Use the materials listed in part 1.

PROCEDURES

1. Draw two or three 9-by-6-inch rectangles on a sheet of drawing paper. (This size is only suggested; make rectangles of whatever size feels comfortable.)

2. With your pencil, begin drawing simple lines, some of which touch each side of the rectangle. In one rectangle you might play with one geometric shape such as a rectangle, triangle, or circle. You can draw freehand or use a ruler if you want. In the other rectangles you might experiment with a free-flowing line drawing, overlapping lines to create new shapes. The point here is to develop a simple dynamic *asymmetrical* or *symmetrical* composition (see figure 1-17). For this project, do not get too complex or too detailed in your design. You will have plenty of opportunity for complexity and detail when you begin applying paint to your design. Later you will choose the drawing you like best out of the three exercises. As you develop your line drawings, keep in mind basic elements of good design listed on pages 32–33.

3. After experimenting with several designs, pick one you really like. Trace it onto a clean piece of Bristol board paper, using your sheet of graphite transfer paper. Place the *graphite sheet face down* on the Bristol board paper. On top of the graphite paper place the drawing paper with the *design face up*. Use several pieces of masking tape to secure all three sheets of paper so they don't move. Next, use a pencil on top of your drawing paper to retrace the lines of your design. When you are finished lift the drawing paper and graphite paper off the Bristol board paper. What you will see is a clean copy of your design on the Bristol board. Save your original design on the drawing paper. You will use it later for experimentation.

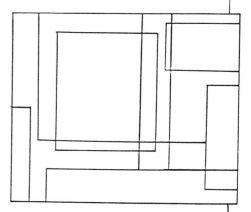

Figure 1-17. *Simple dynamic composition. This picture illustrates repetition and size variation of simple rectangle line drawings. Note that this asymmetrical composition is not complex but includes large, small, and medium rectangles to create interest. Also note that the rectangles are not isolated in the middle of the page, but overlap each other to form new shapes with several lines touching the edges of the frame.*

ACCESSING INSPIRED STATES OF IMAGINATION

I now would like to introduce you to an optional guided visualization that can be used in conjunction with the lessons you just learned on how to create a dynamic line design incorporating elements of good design. This visualization is intended to open you to even deeper states of creativity. It is not absolutely necessary that you do the visualization in order to succeed with this project, because you already have completed a line design. But if you are ready to expand your spiritual consciousness and want to reach higher states of creativity, this visualization will be of great help to you. It will help you create designs from an inspired state of consciousness. You will experience intuition at its highest level—illumination of both the mind and imagination.

If you have never done any guided visualizations, the process may seem quite mysterious to you. Realize, though, that the ability to imagine is one of the greatest human gifts. You may have feared that you had no imaginative abilities until you completed the project outlined above. The guided visualization presented on pages 34–35 is meant to push back the boundaries of your imaginative powers even further and access states normally attributed to genius. If this idea seems too novel for you at present and you find yourself feeling skeptical, leave this visualization exercise for another time and go immediately to the next step in the project.

Ideally, the visualization should be played on a tape player, but if you do not have a tape, ask a friend to read it to you slowly while playing meditative music. Find a quiet place to sit where you will not be distracted. This visualization is designed to help you reach deep inside and discover your higher self or "spiritual guide." This inner guide will take you to what I like to call the Hall of Illumined Arts and Design, where you will see images and designs to inspire your work for the next part of the project.

1. Have a piece of paper and pencil next to you. After you finish the guided visualization, quickly sketch the designs that came to you during the journey and write in detail about the images you saw and what you experienced. If you forget what you imagined, sit quietly and take yourself back to the golden hall to review what you saw.

2. After you have finished, proceed with the project as outlined. Use one of the images you drew to develop as your theme.

Basic Elements of Good Design

Look at the student paintings in figures 1-1, 1-2, and 1-5 of this chapter for examples of symmetrical balance. Designs based on symmetry are arranged on vertical, horizontal, and diagonal axes, all extending from a central point of balance (see figures 1-18 a, b, c). The weight is repeated equally, giving the appearance of stability and certainty. *Horizontal symmetry* means equal weight on top and bottom; *vertical symmetry* means equal weight on both sides. An example from nature is a butterfly with open wings. If you drew a line down the middle of the butterfly's body, you would find equal balance, or vertical symmetry.

Figure 1-18a. Vertical symmetry. This student line drawing illustrates an example of vertical symmetry—that is, the design has equal weight on either side of a vertical axis.

Figures 1-18b and 1-18c. Vertical and horizontal symmetry. These student line drawings illustrate symmetry using both a horizontal and vertical axis. Each of the designs is weighted equally from top to bottom and from side to side.

Figure 1-18a

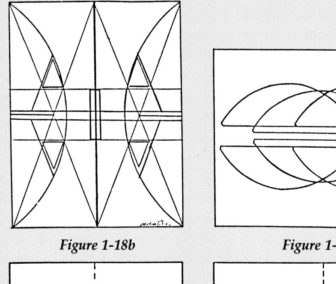

Figure 1-18b

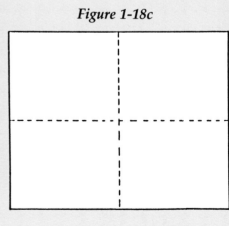

Figure 1-18c

In *asymmetrical balance*, the weight of the design is distributed unevenly and there is a sense of movement and continuously shifting balance. Most of the paintings in this chapter are examples of asymmetrical balance. Standing straight like a soldier with hands at your sides would be an example of symmetrical balance. A ballet dancer standing perfectly balanced on one toe would be an example of asymmetrical balance. Visually, the shift in weight looks dynamic and "feels" correct (see figures 1-19 a, b, c).

Repeating shapes and varying sizes of similar shapes produce interest. Refer to figure 1-17. The latter prevents the repetition of shapes from becoming boring. Think of how many ways you can vary the size of a square or rectangle within a composition by changing its width and length. The temptation, when you are just starting out in art, is to use too many different and unrelated shapes within a composition—combining circles with rectangles and triangles, for example. With experience, new skill, and more visual awareness, you will soon be able to integrate various elements more successfully into a harmonious composition.

Overlap lines and shapes to create new shapes and unite the various separated parts. Draw lines that connect with your frame. The goal is to create a web of connecting shapes and spaces and to avoid isolating and separating various shapes within your composition. Think of a spider's web and how the spider attaches to branches and leaves to produce a beautiful pattern that works as an integrated whole. The web could not be created and suspended in mid-air; so too your design should attach itself in part to the frame.

Line direction creates movement. Do all your lines go in one direction? If so, then the viewer's eye may be directed out of the picture frame. Draw lines and shapes that create interest and direct the eye around, not out of, the picture.

The elements of good design result in harmony and balance. If you sense that your design is boring, simply change it. To create dynamic design, let your imagination open and use your intuition to tell you when it "feels" right. If you start painting when you dislike or feel bored with your design, you will lose interest in completing the project.

Figure 1-19a

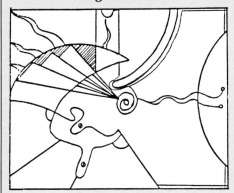

Figure 1-19b

Figure 1-19c

Figures 1-19a, 1-19b, and 1-19c. Asymmetry. These three student line drawings illustrate asymmetrical balance. This type of balance is unequal in weight, but intuitively we know that it "looks" and "feels" right.

The Hall of Illumined Arts and Design

A VISUALIZATION

With your eyes closed, sit comfortably in a chair with your hands resting in your lap and your feet flat on the floor. Imagine at the top of your head a ball or a prism of rainbow light. Now bring that energy down through your head into your brain, down your spine into your lungs, and into your heart. To go on this journey you will need to open up the heart, so at this time I want you to watch as that prism of energy expands. Open your heart, feel a lot of love, and realize that you are wonderful and great. Let the light and love enter your heart; see it filling the whole room in which you are sitting. See how far into the space you can push that energy. Now bring that energy down through your stomach and into your other organs, down through your legs, and into the ground. Feel the stream of warm energy from the top of your head flowing all the way down through your body and into the ground. Now guide that energy up through your feet, up the back of your legs, and bring it slowly up through your spine. And finally, bring it into your head. Imagine the rainbow energy filling your whole being.

You are now ready to go on the journey. Imagine and feel yourself lifting slowly and softly off the ground. Imagine yourself floating effortlessly in the universe among the stars. Feel your weightlessness and see yourself as full of light. Realize that you are a part of this universe, that your physical body was made from all of this stellar energy. Feel peace and love. See yourself turning toward the Earth. See the Earth as the astronauts saw it as they viewed it from the moon: as a blue pearl, beautiful and swirling. You're coming home now . . . come closer to the Earth. See yourself floating above the Earth. Below you is a beautiful forest and a lovely stream. Slowly, gently, drift downward and touch the ground. You are now on the ground. Notice the stream in front of you. Notice how clear the water is. You can look straight to the bottom of the stream—it is so clear and clean. You can see a beautiful reflection of your face on the water. Put your hands into the water. It's so inviting; why don't you take a drink? In your mind's eye, bend over and take a drink from this beautiful stream. As you raise your head, you will notice something bright, like gold, reflecting on the water. Realize that behind you is a gold building somewhere in the forest. You are curious—what could it be?

Arts and Design. As your guide comes closer, open your heart. From your heart, beam a rainbow of light in greeting to this person. Introduce yourself with your name and listen to hear if your guide tells you his or her name.

Follow your guide into this special building. Your guide takes you to a room and points out some designs that you can use in this project . . . and gives you some information on light. Open your imagination to the images that spontaneously come to you.

Listen with your heart and intuition to all that your guide reveals about light. Trust your guide—who is really your higher self—to show and tell you things that will help you create beauty and harmony with light. Open your mind, heart, and spirit to those images of light and design that come to you.

Thank your guide and bid farewell. Follow your guide outside to the clearing by the path in the forest. Walk back through the forest alone, refreshing your memory with the images and knowledge you gained inside the Hall of Illumined Arts and Design. All you imagined and heard with your heart and mind you will bring back with you for inspiration. Lift yourself once more into the universe and feel the abundance of peace and love. Your journey is at an end. See yourself sitting in the chair in the room you left before your journey. You are back now, sitting in your chair in your room. Slowly and gently, when you are ready, open your eyes and in silence write and draw everything you saw.

Get up and turn around to see if you can see it. You see just the tip of the building above the forest and you look for a path. Walk along the stream until you find the path that looks like it will lead to this place. Begin walking through this forest. Notice how the forest feels; notice smells and colors. Feel the peace and love here.

As you continue in the forest, you see a clearing ahead of you and the gold building that you saw reflected partially in the stream. As you approach the clearing, you see a number of people working very hard on various beautiful designs. They are artisans of a very highly evolved culture. They see you and smile at you, inviting you to join them in the clearing in front of the gold building. Watch them for a moment while they work on their designs and art pieces. Looking up, you see a person coming toward you. This person is your special inner guide for the painting you will do later. This guide is a special artisan who has come to show you through the golden Hall of Illumined

If you performed the visualization and became inspired with a design or image, work with it using the following procedures. But don't worry if you came back with no images—repeat the visualization or proceed directly to the project as outlined. Particularly if a person is new to visualization, it takes some practice to activate the imagination and release any abiding fear of creation. So take heart; the visualization will work for you if you practice it.

PROJECT 2: PAINTING WITH LIGHT

PREMIXING YOUR PAINTS BEFORE BEGINNING

1. The next step is to premix your paints. You will premix at least seven values ranging in gradation from darkest charcoal to light gray. Depending on the number of gradations you create, fill seven or more depressions in your mixing tray with white paint. To each depression add various amounts of black to produce a scale similar to the one you made in the first project. When you are finished, fill two other depressions, one with white paint and one with black paint. Use the gray scale in this book and the one you made as a guide. *If you do not prepare your paints ahead of time, you will waste a lot of creative energy trying to mix the scale as you go along. It is important to have all the paints mixed and visually scaled in front of you before you begin.* Have your brush, clean water, and a paper towel nearby. As you paint, you will clean your brush in water each time you use a different color. Use the paper towel to wipe the excess water from your brush.

2. Before you paint on your Bristol board paper, you will experiment with the premixed light scale you made on your drawing paper. Look at your *original design on the drawing paper.* Focus on a small section of your design and look carefully at the shapes created by the lines. Choose three shapes from that section. Paint the entire premixed scale—from white to black—in each of the three shapes on your drawing paper. For small areas, use your small # 1 detail brush. Think of the light scale you are using in terms of music and harmony. As you paint you will notice that you are beginning to get a sense of light and energy. You may wish to draw the small section you have chosen several times so you can experiment. When doing this project, think of

the many ways you can use the full light scale in each section of your design to create dimension, direction, and radiance. Can you use two scales in one shape? What would happen if you started in the center with black first and worked the scale out to white? What would happen if you started with white and worked out to black? Study the student examples to see how others have approached this problem. Refer to the accompanying sidebar for tips on painting technique.

*T*ips on Painting Technique

- Clean your brush each time you use a different color of paint.

- Change your water frequently, as colored water will affect the clarity of your premixed colors.

- Poster paints do not blend on paper the way other media do. So think of each paint as a clear note to be connected to the next. Paint alongside or on top of paints already laid down. If you decide you want to make some changes in your painting, paint your new colors on top of paint that is already dry.

- Check your paints to make sure they are not drying out. Add a few drops of clean water to each section if necessary.

INNER LIGHT: A VISUALIZATION

Before you go on, use the following visualization to relax and center yourself and to raise your consciousness to an illumined state of creativity and intuition. The visualization will put you in touch with your own inner light, which will infuse your work with creative energy. You will recognize this visualization as the introductory part of the journey to the Hall of Illumined Arts and Design. This meditation is used throughout the book to free you from the mundane world and to release the radiant light within you. First put on some music that is inspiring to you. (See the appendix for music suggestions.)

Inner Light
A VISUALIZATION

Ready
yourself for an
experience of the imagination.
Sit upright with your feet flat on the
floor and your hands comfortably in your lap.
Close your eyes and take three deep breaths. On the
exhale, release any tension or negative emotional thoughts
from your body. Imagine a ball of rainbow light at the top of
your head. Imagine it descending into the center of your brain.
Concentrate on that glowing energy and direct it through your neck
and into your heart, feeling warmth and love. Continue directing
it downward—into your stomach and the rest of your organs
and finally through your legs to the soles of your feet and
into the ground. Then visualize this healing and
centering energy coming up from the ground
and up the back of your legs. Slowly
direct it up your spine and
back into your
head.

Sit quietly for a few moments after the visualization and absorb the energy you have created. Your mind, body, and spirit are now focused and you are ready to begin the next part. To keep yourself in a high state of creativity, repeat this exercise every day.

3. After you finish experimenting with the small section on your drawing paper, begin painting the design you traced onto the Bristol board paper. As you work on your design, don't worry about small imperfections or the fact that the poster paint does not lend itself to perfect lines or blending. Let your intuition, inner light, and imagination guide you while you work on your design. Play inspirational music while you work. Keep your mind focused on infusing your design with light and energy. Repeat the visualization if necessary.

4. Take your time with this project. Stand back from your picture occasionally. Hang it up and look at it from a distance. Doing so

will give you a new perspective and will help you use your vision and intuition to decide on ways to incorporate the light scale to create a dynamic luminescent painting.

5. After you have finished, hang up your picture and see if there are any areas you want to change. When you have completed your painting, cut it out and glue it on a clean piece of drawing paper. Be aware that the light and energy you produced in the painting are true reflections of your own beauty and inner light. *Paint, like life, is only gray if you think it is!*

WHAT HAVE YOU LEARNED?

Figure 1-20. Experimenting with the scale of light. These two line drawings show what can happen when the scale is used in various ways within the framework of the same line design. If the design is painted randomly using few gradations of the scale, the result is a flatness in tone. A sense of light is created when you use a logical progression of values in repeated and creative ways.

Whether you did this project alone, with friends, or in a classroom, the following considerations will help you learn more about both your creative power and the ideas or convictions that can block your creativity.

There has been much discussion recently of our dual brain, with its right and left hemispheres and its untapped potential. But we must remind ourselves that brain research is a young science, and the right/left cognitive delineations should not be taken as dogma, for even the researchers do not agree among themselves. Calling logic, reason, and Western language left-brain skills and the creative abilities to see color and pictures, hear sounds, imagine, and be intuitive exclusively functions of the right brain might in the long run inhibit an accurate understanding of how these functions actually occur. I use the terms here more as metaphors than actual phenomena in order to distinguish among our different ways of knowing, perceiving, and problem solving. In this context, it is certainly safe to state as fact that we have developed predominantly the analytical side of ourselves to the exclusion of the creative functions. Intellect, reason, and logic have been nurtured and reinforced in our society, whereas creativity and intuition often are ignored.

If you were to have approached this project simply by reading the chapter and accepting it as logical and reasonable, memorizing the information so you could reiterate the procedures, you would have been demonstrating the analytical approach to problem solving. If quizzed about the gray scale—its function and appearance—you would be able to discuss it intelligently. But let me ask you a couple of questions:

• Even though this chapter sounded logical and you saw proof from illustrations that black-and-white paint could take on the appearance of light and energy, could you be absolutely sure that the information in this chapter was correct without actually mixing the paint yourself and changing your consciousness through visualizations?

• Using only a verbal or written articulation of the material presented in this chapter, would you be able to come up with an original design and painting?

In order to actually do this project, you had to use the logical steps outlined in the procedures, but this logical process led you to experiential knowledge. It was through actual experimentation that you confirmed the truth of the logic. By actually mixing black-and-white paints together you learned firsthand exactly how these paints combine to produce a series of grays. Then you had to use your right-brain skills of intuition and imagination. You had to train your mind to focus inward on your inner light. You used visualizations to release fears, open your heart to love, and thereby change your perception of gray to one of light. You developed a new definition of physical reality as being composed of integrated electromagnetic energies. All in all, you used more than logic and reason. You integrated your mind, body, and spirit.

• In doing this project, what did you learn about your own creative capacity? Did you exceed your initial expectations for achievement?

• Think about the fears you had to overcome: fear of failure, fear of commitment, and so forth. Are these also the fears that hold you back in your everyday life? Could you bring the peaceful certainty of your visualizations to your daily activities? Do you believe that love and untapped knowledge within you can help you to create a more joyous and beautiful world for yourself?

• Let us consider the word *gray*. Before you changed your focus, the definition you assigned to the word *gray* influenced your view of reality and the way you used black-and-white paints. *Your belief system had to change* before you could produce radiance and light. If this statement is true, then how many words do you use every day that influence your life in a negative way, blocking you from realizing your creative potential and experiencing a better life? List a few words that you use continuously that create a negative self-image. If you can't think of any, ask friends who listen to you all the time to point out the negative words in your vocabulary.

▪ Next to the words you listed, write down words that are opposite and affirmative. For example, if you say "I can't," write down "I can." Next to "I have no talent," write "I have undreamed-of talent." Work on using these new positive words in your vocabulary every day. You may discover that you are surrounding yourself with people whose negative views are helping you to create your poor self-image. Perhaps you should love yourself enough to seek out new friends and environments that nurture a positive self-image.

Make a joyful commitment to your own creative development! You may be inspired by the pictures in this chapter, but if you only read and look at the pictures you cannot tap the deeper knowledge and power that is available to you through experiential learning. Change is continual in our universe. To stay where you are, resisting change means to resist the natural, creative flow of the universe to which you are intimately bonded. The next chapter will lead you even deeper into creatively expressing the beauty and light that resides in you.

SUGGESTED READING

Birren, Faber. *Creative Color.* New York: Van Nostrand Reinhold, 1961.

Kohn, Alfie. *No Contest: The Case Against Competition.* Boston: Houghton Mifflin, 1986.

Los Angeles County Museum of Art. *The Spiritual in Art: Abstract Painting 1890–1985.* New York: Abbeville Press, 1986.

Regier, Kathleen J., comp. *The Spiritual Image in Modern Art.* Wheaton, Ill.: Theosophical Publishing House, 1987.

Roman, Sanaya. *Living with Joy: Keys to Personal Power & Spiritual Transformation.* Tiburon, Calif.: H. J. Kramer, 1986.

NOTES

1. David V. Erdman, *The Poetry and Prose of William Blake* (New York: Doubleday, 1965), 201.

## CHAPTER 2

The Joy of Luminescent Color

Within a man of light there is light and he lights the whole world. When he does not shine, there is darkness.

—The Gospel According to Thomas, Log. 24[1]

The illusion of luminosity in art is one of the highest expressions possible with color. . . it is rare among all color achievements.

—Faber Birren, *Creative Color*[2]

If man is awed by what he sees in his surroundings, he should be far more impressed by what lies within the sancturary of his own being.

—Faber Birren[3]

COLOR IS ONE of the most magnificent experiences in which you can involve yourself. You may respond with awe and wonder at the paintings in color insert 1. For me they invoke a sense of luminescent splendor, reflecting the inner life of the individuals who made them. Mystical, magical, and mysterious, these paintings reveal their artists' hidden world of color and light. These inspiring works, done by people with little or no color or painting experience, demonstrate that anyone committed to learning, changing consciousness, and opening the heart to the love, light, and knowledge within can participate fully in the ongoing creation of the universe.

Whether your only experience in painting has been the project in chapter 1 or you've been a practicing artist for some time, or even if you have skipped chapter 1 and have never lifted a paintbrush before, it is important to understand that the pictures in this chapter go beyond the normal everyday sensory perceptions of light and color. In traditional approaches artists seek inspiration and knowledge of light and color from natural phenomena, but in this chapter you will first learn traditional color-mixing procedures and then apply them in expressing your own *inner* light. Study the student work here and you'll see that everyone used the same colors but each achieved a highly original expression of light as a result of his or her individuality, intuition, and inner search for knowledge.

If you are like most people, you probably learned little or nothing about color mixing in school. You might be intimidated by the pictures here, thinking you could never produce anything nearly as beautiful and inspiring. You would not be the first to feel such insecurity. When I show student work to my classes, most people do not believe they can do anything as beautiful or as original. Tom, a former design student, speaks for the many students who experience this initial fear when I ask them to create an original luminescent painting of the color wheel (see figure C1-12):

> When I saw the color wheels by other students, I felt panic. I thought, "There is no way that I am going to be able to do anything like what these people did. I just don't have the training." This is what I kept thinking, because in my previous educational experience, the idea was, "This is the way you learn because we set up rules for you and you learn in this fashion." But now all of a sudden I had a teacher who

was saying, "No, I'm not going to give you rules, but you're going to be able to do this. Trust me." I was afraid because Judith wasn't giving us a set of rules to work with. She had us reach within ourselves—and it was there . . . and I let it flow outward. It was a very frightening experience, especially when people around me were saying, "Oh no, there must be a certain way you've got to do it." When I ignored the other people and let it flow out, all of a sudden I created something. I could look at it and say, "Hey, I can do something on my own."

I have taught hundreds of people like Tom who have had no experience, and *not one* design has ever been duplicated. Everyone, including yourself, is unique and special. The last project in this chapter is designed to guide you inward and enable you to express your unique spiritual beauty in luminescent color.

At the same time, the chapter teaches you the essentials of mixing and handling color pigments. Sometimes my beginning students say that they feel they ought to know all about color before they take the class and that they ought to be able to paint as soon as they buy their paints. But color harmony, like music, is a complex phenomenon. If you wanted to play music without knowing scales and picked up a violin that was not tuned, could you play beautiful music? Color is the same way. To create a beautiful painting you need to learn about color harmony before you begin. If you are like some I have taught, you might be concerned that disciplined study will ruin your spontaneity with regard to painting, but I can assure you that this is not so. Great musicians of the past and present knew their scales and practiced their art. Knowledge freed them to express their artistry profoundly; this is also true in painting. This chapter will teach you some basic principles of color and then guide you in shaping that knowledge with your intuition and inner light.

A NOTE ON COLOR PERMANENCY IN PAINT PIGMENTS

Color permanency in paint is an important issue. The permanency of colors in paint depends on how the paint has been manufactured and what ingredients have been used in it. The colors used in a painting should be able to withstand normal lighting conditions in the home for many years of exposure without fading. A few of the designer gouaches you will be using in this project are not as color-permanent as oils, acrylics, or transparent watercolors. But they are inexpensive, easy to use, and easy to clean up compared with other paint media, and the handling of the others requires more technical expertise. Designer gouaches are used by professional illustrators and graphic design artists. After you finish this project, feel free to explore other paint media using the color wheel you create as a guide to buying colors that are harmonious with the prismatic spectrum. But *check the manufacturer's codes for color permanency* if you are going to invest a lot of money on art supplies and a lot of time developing your skills professionally, since *not all oil, acrylic, and transparent watercolor paints are permanent.* As a professional artist, I look for colors in oils and watercolors that are in harmony with the Ives color wheel discussed here and that are considered fairly permanent.

If you are a professional artist and want to do this project in your own medium, I would suggest you try thalo greens and blues, which can be blended into a nice turquoise. Experiment with magenta and synthetic quinacridone reds and red violets along with your thalo blue and green. Many manufacturers make magenta or thalo reds, blues, and greens, but just because they are all labeled the same does not mean that they are the same. Labeling can be deceiving and paints from different companies can vary widely in color clarity and their ability to blend in a harmonious prismatic scale. You will need to experiment with actual colors to develop a harmonious blend.

If this is your first color experience, don't worry about experimenting with colors. You need only to choose a set of colors I have listed under Materials. They are the same colors used by the students whose paintings appear in this chapter (see color insert, figures C1-1–C1-18).

PART 1: LEARNING ABOUT COLOR

Learning about color should be a joyful experience. While you follow the procedures in the following exercise, pay careful attention to what it is you are handling. Color can affect you on many levels: emotionally, physically, mentally, and spiritually. Notice how each color makes you feel as you work with it. Which colors attract you emotionally and visually? Some colors may feel warm and others cool. As you paint the different colors, notice that each color pigment has different physical properties and therefore will handle differently.

To make working with color an even greater learning experience, you might consider working with a group of friends. Part of the fun is learning from one another. You will find that every person will approach painting differently and come up with unique solutions for light and color problems. And through cooperative learning and sharing of talents, you are sure to progress more quickly. If you have a lot of ingrained fears, a group can ease you past them—and you must find a way past them if you are to create. You can remind each other to be positive and loving when you slip into negative thoughts, fear, and doubt about your ability to succeed.

BASIC COLOR CONCEPTS

This first exercise will teach you about primary, secondary, and tertiary color mixing of paint pigments. You will learn firsthand that *blue and yellow paint mixed together make greens,* that *magenta and yellow mixed together make reds and oranges,* and that *magenta and blue mixed together make red-violets, violets, and blue-violets.* When ordered in logical sequence, these colors produce a rainbow spectrum in paints, similar to a rainbow made of diffracted visible light. You will also learn how to create a richer palette by adding premixed secondary colors to your primary colors and to create a traditional color wheel. Making a color wheel is important because it will give you a deep experiential understanding of colored pigments. By making a color wheel you will learn the logical order of mixing color. You will use this color wheel as a reference for part 3 of this project, in which you will paint a design using the full spectrum of color.

PRIMARY COLORS OF VISIBLE LIGHT

The sight of white light broken into its various colors, as in the rainbow or a prism, is the closest we come to perceiving the divine or spiritual in natural phenomena through our senses. The primary colors of this visible light are *red, green,* and *blue-violet.* When these three colors of light rays overlap, the colors *combine to create white light.* Secondary colors are produced from visible light when red and green light overlap to produce yellow, green overlaps with blue-violet to produce turquoise, and red overlaps with blue-violet to produce magenta.

The first color wheel of visible light was developed by Sir Isaac Newton in about 1666. When he directed visible light through a prism he discovered that a spectrum of pure colors was formed: red through orange, yellow, green, blue, and violet. Purple was missing from the visible light spectrum, but purple, he found, is formed when the red and violet ends of the spectrum are brought together. This discovery gave Isaac Newton the idea to chart colors of visible light in the form of a circle (see figure C1-14).

PRIMARY COLORS OF PIGMENTS

A theory of primary colors for pigments evolved after Isaac Newton's discovery. Around 1731, Frenchman J. C. LeBlon put forth a color theory stating that the primary colors for pigments were red, yellow, and blue. What LeBlon discovered was immediately applied to painting, printmaking, and engraving. However, he did not develop a well-organized color circle. That was developed later by Moses Harris, an Englishman. In 1766, Harris published *The Natural Systems of Color* illustrating a prismatic color wheel for paint pigments.

The primary colors you will be using in paints to make a harmonious color wheel are *magenta, yellow,* and *turquoise* (see figure C1-15). The three primary colors I have chosen for paint pigments are similar to the secondary colors produced from the visible light spectrum when red, green, and blue-violet overlap (see figure C1-14). *I am talking about two different types of color here.* The first is the color of visible light rays known most commonly as the rainbow spectrum when it is broken into its various colors. The second is the color of paint pigments made to approximate the colors of the rainbow spectrum. When these pigment colors—magenta, yellow, and turquoise blue—are intermixed with each other in the right logical order, they result in a color wheel, a harmonious rainbow spectrum of colored paint pigments (see figure C1-16).

SECONDARY COLORS OF PIGMENTS

Yellow, magenta, and turquoise are called primary colors, because they are the fewest colors needed in pigment mixing to produce the secondary and tertiary colors of greens, oranges, reds, and violets—the other colors of the rainbow spectrum. To make a richer color wheel you will be adding three other colors: *orange, green,* and *violet.* You could make these secondary colors with just the three primary colors, but your color wheel will be richer and more vibrant if you add premixed secondary colors to your palette.

If you have already had some training in color mixing, you may be surprised at my choice of primary colors for this project. Traditionally, a red containing no blue (magenta does contain blue), a yellow, and a blue containing no green (turquoise does contain green) are used as the primary pigment colors. But in the course of my teaching and painting experience, I came to reject these traditional choices in favor of the colors used here. My reasons are rooted in results, not convention, since the actual mixing of the traditional primaries yields not beautiful purples and violets but a muddy red to brownish blue, a very unharmonious color blend.

However, a color wheel devised by American colorist Herbert Ives yields great harmony and beauty in the mixing of pigments, and the primary colors he used for pigments and dyes were magenta, yellow, and turquoise. As you will discover, the paint spectrum resulting from these colors closely resembles the natural rainbow spectrum. If we are going to try to achieve the effects of light and luminescence with paints, it stands to reason that the pigment colors we start with must be tuned visually to the visible light spectrum, because that spectrum is not only visible to our eyes but emotionally evokes in us the spiritual nature.

PROJECT 1: CREATING A RAINBOW SPECTRUM WITH PAINT

MATERIALS

Designer gouache comes in a number of brands. Rather than list them all, I have noted one that is available in most art supply stores. If you want to experiment with other brands, look for turquoise, magenta, and brilliant yellow to use as your primary mixing colors. To make it easy, take the materials list with you to the art store.

If you want to do this exercise with children, I suggest you buy the same colors in premixed tempera paints.

- Winsor and Newton designer gouache: magenta (or you can use rose tyrien; I find this color a bit more vibrant and closer to the magenta that printers use in four-color separation), spectrum yellow, turquoise blue (or you can use peacock blue; this also is a bit more vibrant as a turquoise color), orange lake light, brilliant green, spectrum violet
- 14-by-17-inch Bristol board pad—smooth texture, medium weight
- One sheet of 14-by-17-inch drawing paper
- Compass
- Protractor
- Pencil
- Ruler
- Scissors
- Water container
- High-quality # 6 sable watercolor brush
- Plastic mixing tray that can hold twelve or more mixed pigments
- Rubber cement
- Paper towels
- Inspirational music

Audio tapes of the guided visualizations for the exercises in this book can be obtained by contacting Manifesting Inner Light. See the Appendix, page 211.

PROCEDURES

In this preliminary exercise, you will be approximating a rainbow spectrum—the visible colors of white light broken down—using three primary colors of paint pigments.

1. Take out your three primary colors—magenta, yellow, and turquoise—and your water container, brush, paint tray, and a sheet of Bristol board paper. In this first exercise you will learn why primary colors mix with each other to form a rainbow spectrum. You will not be saving this exercise to cut for your color wheel, so you can proceed quite rapidly without worrying about the width of your strokes.

2. Fill one of the depressions in your mixing tray with magenta paint and one with yellow paint. Check to see that your colors are smooth and creamy, not stiff in texture. If a color is stiff, add a little water and mix it with your brush until it is creamy and smooth. When you apply it, it should flow evenly onto the paper. If paint chips off the paper after it has dried, it was probably too stiff and thick. If your color looks transparent on the paper, you have added too much water. Remember that you are using opaque colors, not transparent water colors. Through practice in mixing these colors, you will learn how much water to use.

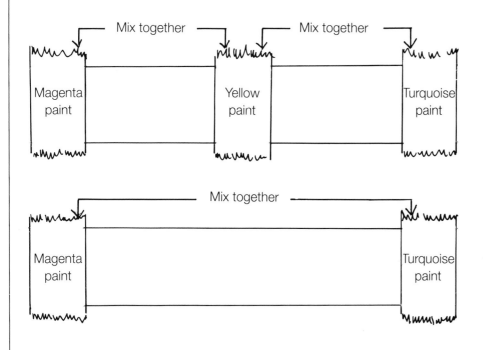

Figure 2-1. With your paper in a horizontal position, take a pencil and draw two horizontal lines that are parallel to each other. Paint a band of yellow in the middle of the top line. On the far left side, paint a band of magenta on the top and the bottom line. On the right side of the paper, paint a band of turquoise on the top and bottom lines. Then follow the directions for Project 1: Creating a Rainbow Spectrum with Paint.

3. With your paper lying in a horizontal position, paint a band of yellow in the middle of the paper, near the top of the page. Clean your brush thoroughly. Next paint a band of magenta on the left side of the paper near the upper edge. Rinse your brush and take off excess water with a paper towel. You will start by mixing magenta into the yellow, but if your brush is full of magenta to begin with, your transitions from yellow-oranges to reds will be too abrupt.

4. Take a small amount of magenta on your brush, put it into the yellow in your mixing tray, and mix it well. You will notice little color change. Paint the mixture next to the yellow paint on your paper. Next, put more magenta on your brush and mix it again into the yellow paint. Paint the mixture next to the one you just did. Continue mixing in this manner and create a nice color range from yellow, through a series of yellow-oranges, to orange, through reds, and back to magenta. Clean your brush thoroughly and change your water when you have completed this step.

5. Fill two clean depressions in your mixing tray, one with yellow and one with turquoise blue. You won't need to paint a yellow band this time, since you already did it in the last exercise. Take some turquoise blue on your brush and on the far right-hand side of the paper paint a strip of blue near the top edge. Rinse your brush and wipe off the excess water. Put a small amount of turquoise blue on your brush and mix it into the yellow paint in your paint tray. Paint a strip of this mixture next to the yellow on the side facing the turquoise blue. Take more turquoise on your brush, mixing it again into the yellow. Paint this mixture next to your last mixture by the yellow. Continue mixing in this manner, creating a color range from yellow-greens, to greens, back to blue. Clean your brush thoroughly and change your water when you have completed this step.

6. Fill two clean depressions in your mixing tray, one with magenta and one with turquoise blue. Take a small amount of turquoise on your brush and mix it into your magenta. Paint this color under your magenta strip on the left side of the paper. Take a little more turquoise and again mix it into the magenta, painting this next to the last strip you painted. Continue mixing and painting in this manner, working across the page toward the blue. Create a color range that proceeds from magenta, through red-violets, violets, blue-violets, and back to blue. If

you look at what you have just completed, you will see the logic and order of color mixing and that you have just created a rainbow spectrum from your primary colors. After this exercise, wash your paint tray and brush thoroughly and change your water. *Do not let your brushes stand in water on the bristles or they will bend out of shape. After you have washed a brush, pull your fingers over the top of the bristles, moving toward the point. Doing so will keep your brush pointed and prevent the bristles from becoming spread out.*

PROJECT 2: CREATING A SIMPLE COLOR WHEEL

Now that you understand primary mixes, you will add the premixed secondary colors orange, green, and violet to your primary colors to produce a richer, more vibrant color palette. In this exercise you will be cutting paint strips out of your Bristol board. You'll cut out and glue to a clean sheet of paper the six premixed primary and secondary colors along with six tertiary colors (colors formed by mixing primary and secondary colors together) in order to create a simple color wheel. The strips you paint in this exercise need not be wider or longer than three-quarters of an inch to an inch. You will use this color wheel later as reference for your final painting.

TERTIARY COLORS OF PIGMENTS

Tertiary colors are those colors that fall between the primary and secondary color mixes. Since we are using the Ives color wheel, your tertiary mix between magenta and orange will be *red.* The tertiary color between orange and yellow will be *yellow-orange.* The tertiary color between yellow and green will be *yellow-green* and between green and blue it will be *blue-green.* The tertiary mix between blue and violet will be *blue-violet,* and between violet and magenta will be *red-violet.* For your final painting you will be using the following twelve colors composed of primary, secondary, and tertiary mixes: magenta, red, orange, yellow-orange, yellow, yellow-green, green, blue-green, turquoise, blue-violet, violet, and red-violet.

You will end up with many more gradations of color from intermixing the primary and secondary colors than the twelve you will be using in your final project. Part of this exercise is to teach you how few colors you actually need to make a multitude of combinations without resorting to buying many tubes of paint.

*PROCEDURES FOR MIXING PRIMARY AND
SECONDARY COLORS*

1. Fill one depression in your mixing tray with magenta and one with orange. Place a clean piece of Bristol board paper vertically in front of you, and paint a strip of orange at the top right corner. Clean your brush. Put some magenta on your brush and paint a strip of magenta at the top left corner of the paper. Clean your brush. Take a small bit of magenta and mix it into the orange paint. Paint this first mixture next to the orange. Continue with this process, mixing the magenta into the orange and painting strips next to the previous one. Create a scale going from orange through red-oranges to reds and back to magenta. Clean your brush and change the water. See figure C1-18 of the color insert.

2. Fill a clean depression in your tray with orange and one with yellow. Paint a strip of yellow underneath the magenta on the left side of the paper. Clean your brush. Put a small amount of orange on the brush and mix it into the yellow. Paint this mixture next to the yellow. Continue working this way by mixing orange into the yellow until you have a nice progression going back to orange. *Each time you proceed to another color mix, clean your brush and use clean water.*

3. Fill one clean depression with yellow and one with green. Paint a green strip on the right side of the paper, leaving a small space between it and the orange. Clean your brush. Put a small amount of green on your brush and mix it into the yellow, and paint this mixture underneath the yellow. Continue working in this manner until you have a series going from yellow-greens back to green. If at any time you get confused just refer to figure C1-18.

4. Fill one clean depression with green and one with turquoise blue. Paint a strip of blue on the left side of the paper, leaving a small space between it and your yellow. Clean your brush. Put a small amount of blue on your brush and mix it into your green, painting this mixture underneath your green strip. Continue in this manner working back from green through blue-greens to your turquoise blue.

5. Fill one clean depression with turquoise and one with violet. Paint a strip of violet on the right side of your paper, leaving a small space between it and the green. Clean your brush. Put a

small amount of violet on your brush and mix it into your blue. Paint this mixture underneath your blue strip. Continue working in this manner creating transitions from blue to blue-violets and back to violet.

6. Fill one depression with turquoise and one with magenta. Paint a strip of magenta under your turquoise. Clean your brush. Put a small amount of violet on your brush and mix it into the magenta, painting this mixture next to the magenta. Continue in this manner, creating transitions from magenta to red-violets leading back to violet. Let the paint dry while you go to the next step in creating your color wheel.

PROCEDURES FOR CONSTRUCTING A COLOR WHEEL

1. Take out a clean sheet of drawing paper, pencil, compass, ruler, protractor, scissors, and glue. Set your compass at three-and-a-half inches. Draw a circle in the middle of your drawing paper using your compass. Your circle should be approximately seven inches in diameter.

2. Divide your circle into twelve equal sections using your protractor and marking a dot at every 30-degree increment with your pencil. Place your protractor in the middle of the circle you have drawn. The arrow or dot marking the middle on the flat edge of the protractor should be lined up on the point in the center of your circle. This center point was made by the compass when it pressed into the paper. Hold the protractor in position and make a pencil dot next to the following degrees on your protractor: zero, 30, 60, 90, 120, 150, 180. When you finish, turn the protractor upside down. Again, center the middle of the protractor with the point in the middle of the circle. Line up the zero and 180 degrees marked on the protractor with the two pencil dots you just marked on your paper for the zero and 180 degrees. To complete marking your dots for your twelve-division circle, you need only mark 30, 60, 90, 120, and 150 degrees, since you already marked the zero and 180. Using your ruler, draw a pencil line from each dot to the center of the circle. The line should begin at the circle's edge and run through the dot mark ending in the center dot of the circle. When you finish, your circle should be divided in twelve equal sections. See figure 2-2 for a line drawing of a color wheel.

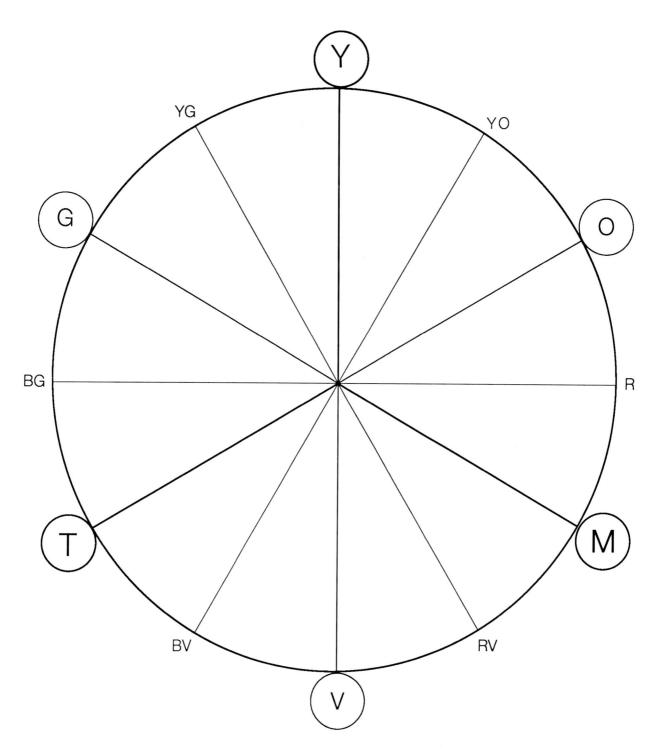

Figure 2-2. *This circle is divided into twelve sections and labeled according to color theoriest Herbert Ives' conception of the logical order and progression of spectrum colors. Y stands for yellow, M stands for magenta, T stands for turquoise blue—the primary colors and their positions on the twelve-division color wheel. G stands for green, O stands for orange, V stands for violet—the secondary colors and their correct position between colors on the color wheel. R stands for red, YO stands for yellow-orange, YG stands for yellow-green, BG stands for blue-green, BV stands for blue-violet, RV stands for red-violet—the tertiary colors in their correct positions on the color wheel.*

3. Take out the Bristol board sheet on which you mixed both secondary and primary colors together. First you will cut out your primary colors: magenta, yellow, and turquoise. Decide on a shape you will make them, such as a circle or a square. Make their shapes as large as possible as a reminder to you that they represent your primary colors. Draw the shape in pencil on top of the painted magenta, yellow, and turquoise. When you finish, cut out the shapes and use your rubber cement to glue them in the right order on the outer edge of your circle. Label lightly in pencil the names and correct order for the twelve color divisions before you begin. For guidance see figure C1-16.

4. Next, cut out your secondary colors: green, orange, and violet. You might make these shapes slightly smaller or of a different shape to remind you that they are secondary mixes. Cut them out and glue them in the correct order. If you have done this procedure correctly, you will have only one space left between each of the colors. These spaces are for your tertiary colors.

5. Next cut out your tertiary colors: red, yellow-orange, yellow-green, blue-green, blue-violet, and red-violet. Decide on a shape for these colors and draw it on top of your paint colors. Cut them out and arrange them in the correct order on the color wheel. *Before you glue them down, check to make sure that each color creates a logical transition* between your primary and secondary mixes. For example, look at the yellow and green colors that you glued down and the yellow-green you chose to go in between. Make sure your yellow-green is not too close in transition either to the green or to the yellow but that it gives a visual sense of being in the middle between the two colors. If you find that what you chose is too close to either of the colors, go back to your paint samples and cut out one that reflects this middle or tertiary mix. When you have checked all the tertiaries for visual harmony and logical transition, glue them onto your color wheel.

6. Now that you have completed constructing your color wheel, label each color according to primary, secondary, and tertiary mixes so that you don't forget how they were mixed.

WHAT HAVE YOU LEARNED?

Before proceeding to the next part, take a few minutes to review what you have learned about color so far. We live in a world of color, but for the most part we are unaware of how colors affect us emotionally. Some colors can appear warm whereas others give us a cool sensation. As you become more conscious of color, look at your environment and at the clothes you wear. Are there colors around you that you have ignored? In doing this exercise, did you discover that you really did not like a particular color?

- What colors felt like warm colors to you? List them. Of the warm colors you listed, which color or colors were you most attracted to? Did any colors make you feel uncomfortable? Are those colors in your environment or in the clothes you wear?

- What colors felt cool to you? List them. Of the cool colors, to which were you most attracted? Least attracted? Are these colors in your surroundings? Which colors would you like to remove from or add to your environment?

- When you were mixing the colors, did you notice the individual energy and life that each color seems to have? If you did not, try to be more conscious as you complete the problems in this chapter.

PART 2: TINTS, TONES, AND SHADES AS SCALES OF LIGHT AND ENERGY

In chapter 1 you learned about mixing black-and-white paint to create a scale of light. In part 2 you will learn to mix other scales of light by mixing individual pure colors into black-and-white paints. You'll then apply the knowledge you will gain from this exercise to your final painting. These new scales will afford you even greater possibilities for expressing your inner light.

There are three exercises to this part: (1) creating a scale of tints by mixing color with white; (2) creating a scale of shades by mixing color with black; and (3) creating various tone scales by mixing color into the various mixtures of black and white, using the scale you created in chapter 1 as reference.

MATERIALS

- Choose one favorite color from your selection of three primary or three secondary paint colors. You will work with only one color, plus black and white, for this project.
- High-quality poster paint or designer gouache—jar of white and small container of jet black
- Your 9-by-12-inch divided rectangle with the black-and-white scale that you completed in chapter 1
- Your 3-by-3-inch template used in chapter 1 to trace squares
- High-quality # 6 sable watercolor brush
- 14-by-17-inch Bristol board pad—smooth texture, medium weight
- Pencil
- Ruler
- Scissors
- Water container
- Rubber cement
- Plastic mixing tray
- Paper towels
- Inspirational music

EXERCISE 1: CREATING A TINT

1. Before you begin, do the inner-light visualization from chapter 1 (pages 38–39). This exercise will help you to relax and open the door to your creative potential. When you have finished, take out the pure color you have chosen, your white paint, brush, mixing tray, water container, and a clean sheet of Bristol board paper (see figure C1-17 of completed rectangle using tints, tones, and shades).

2. Fill two depressions in your mixing tray with white and one with the color you chose. Put a small amount of pure color on your brush and mix it into the white paint. Paint a band of this mixture on your Bristol board wide enough so that you will be able to cut an inch square from it. Put some more color on your brush and mix it well into the white paint. Paint this mixture next to the one you just painted. Continue working in this manner, creating a series of tints going from light to deep rich tints. Clean your brush. Paint a pure band of the color you are using onto the Bristol board.

3. Take out the original 9-by-12-inch rectangle containing your scale of light. At the top of the scale is a square of white paint and four empty squares. In these four squares you will paste four of the tints that show a nice transition, starting with light tints next to the white, working back to a deep rich tint.

4. Choose four tints from the selection you have painted that you think would make a nice transitional series. Using your square template, draw a square on top of your choices. Cut them out and arrange them horizontally at the top of your light scale, starting with the lightest tint next to your white and working back. Check them again before you paste them down to make sure that they make a nice logical transition.

5. Cut a square of the pure color you painted. Paste it next to the last tint you glued down, just outside the rectangle. It will serve as a color key to remind you later that you used this particular color throughout all three exercises.

EXERCISE 2: CREATING A SHADE

1. You will now learn how to mix shades by adding black to your color; refer to figure C1-17. Fill two depressions in your tray, one with black and one with your pure color. Using a clean brush, take a very small amount of black on your brush and mix it into your color. Using the same sheet of Bristol board, paint a strip of this mixture on the left-hand side under your tints. Take a bit more black on your brush and again mix it into your color and paint it next to your last band. Continue painting this way until you find your color is almost pure black. In mixing shades you will find that your scale transition in creating shades tends to be much shorter than in mixing tints, especially when you mix your darker colors like violet and blue with black. Remember that black really absorbs color, and the more black you add, the less color you will see. It takes a very small addition of black to your pure color to get a new shade variation. Think of shades as deep dark notes on a scale and remember that very little goes a long way. With tints, however, you could create a long scale with many variations. The exception is when you use yellow with white. Because yellow is so close to the intensity of white, you will find that the yellow tint scale will have less visible variation and length in the scale. Think of tints as light high notes in a scale.

2. When you are finished, select and cut out four shades that show a logical transition going from dark shades to one that has mostly color and very little black in it. At the bottom of your 9-by-12-inch rectangle is your square of black paint. Line up your four shades, starting with your darkest. Next go to your black and work across to the one that is mostly color with very little black. Glue them down with rubber cement. So far you have completed the tints or lighter scale using white plus color and a dark deep scale of shades using black plus color. Clean your brush and change your water.

EXERCISE 3: CREATING A TONE

1. You will now learn how to mix tones using black and white plus color. Look at your scale of light. You will notice that you have seven scales of light going from white with little black in it to deep charcoal or black with little white in it. From each of these gradations you will create new tone scales. Working at the lightest end first, in one of the depressions in your paint tray mix black and white together to make your lightest gray. In another depression put your pure color. Put some color on your brush and mix it into the gray and paint a band of this on your Bristol board. Again put color on your brush and mix it into the light gray. Paint a band of this on your Bristol board. Continue in this manner until you have saturated the light gray with mostly color.

2. From these bands you will choose and cut out four tones that show a transition from mostly gray with little color to mostly color with little gray. Lay down the tone square with the greatest amount of gray in it next to your lightest gray on the scale, following with tones that become more and more saturated with color. Paste these down. Go on to the next darker gray on the light scale, repeating the same procedure by mixing the black and white first and then adding additions of color to saturate it. Repeat this procedure for each of the seven scales or combinations of black-and-white paint mixes. When you have finished, cut them out and glue them down in the right order (see figure C1-17 of completed rectangle using tints, tones, and shades). Label your new scales (tints, tones, and shades) so you will remember what you did and what they are called.

WHAT HAVE YOU LEARNED?

Look at the rectangle you have just completed by creating tints, tones, and shades. By using just one pure color plus black-and-white paint, you were able to create a whole new range of scales. In part 3 you will use these scales to do your final luminescent painting. Cover your black-and-white scale of light with a piece of paper so that all you see are the new scales you just created. When you look at it in this way, you will notice that the lightest or brightest scale is the tint scale. It is followed by numerous progressions of soft to deep rich tone scales, which in turn is followed by the dark, rich shade scale.

Your tones offer you the most complexity and variety, for each gray takes on a scale of light within itself, depending on the amount of pure color you add to it. You might think of tones as muted soft sounds of music, which when played (painted) in conjunction with the higher, clearer, brighter scales of tints, suppress or mute the painting field around them so that the tints appear to come forward and glow more clearly and brightly. The shades, on the other hand, have a deep mysterious light even more muted than the tones. Shades used in conjunction with rich tones act as a dark field that has the effect of pushing the tones forward, making them seem to glow even more.

Now that you have completed the procedures for mixing pure colors with black-and-white paint to create new scales, study the paintings that illustrate this chapter, found in the color insert (figures C1-1 through C1-12). You should have a new awareness and appreciation for these pictures now. See if you can identify where tints, tones, shades, and pure color were used in the pictures. But also pay attention to the wonderful diversity represented in this array of paintings and be aware that you now possess the tools to add to this gallery of luminescent pictures. I have made comments on a few of these pictures. These comments are intended only as a guide to help you study with more appreciation the work that is presented.

ANALYSIS OF PAINTINGS

Beyoung created a powerful painting (see figure C1-9) that goes beyond the use of ordinary pigments. His composition is scaled with a large amount of pure color, starting with deep purple bands going into yellow-orange and picking up again in the center diamond shape with oranges, reds, magenta, and back again to the violet. His triangles contain scales of tints and tones. Usually when a person uses this much pure color, the effect is too raw. But with Beyoung's mind and heart centered on his inner light, he was able to produce a highly sophisticated, mystical, and powerful painting. Although he used the circle as his theme, he did not divide it the way the other students did. Instead he created a vertically symmetrical piece, radiating his color outward from small to larger circles and triangles. In the process of creating his painting, Beyoung not only learned about color and light but he also gained access to the beauty and light that is within all of us.

Karen used only tones, tints, and pure colors, avoiding shades altogether in her painting (see figure C1-6). She created an inventively simple geometric composition with a star design in the middle in which she painted pure colors in logical order. The rest of the design came to life with light through the subtle use and directional movement of tints and tones. The effect is a splendid three-dimensional illusion of luminescent light moving forward and backward. Karen experimented with several possibilities for scales and directional movements on her original drawing before doing her final painting.

Like a spiraling corona, Michelle's painting evokes a sensation of the universe as it expands into a galaxy of color, light, and intelligence, born out of the depths of darkness (see figure C1-4). Starting with a pure black center, Michelle leads the viewer out of this darkness into light—and life. She starts with pure colors, goes into shades and tones, and expands this swirling sensation of light with the use of warm, rich tints and tones at the outer edge of the corona spiraling off the paper. Her painting appears simple in concept and execution, but it is a powerful, elegant, joyous movement of light.

Robert (see figure C1-5) started in the center with tints leading to pure color, deep tones, and dark shades going into blackness. The effect is a center of light within darkness with the viewer pulled magnetically inward toward the mystery of light at the center. By contrast, in Michelle's painting (figure C1-4) the viewer is forced out of the center, which is dark, into the infinite expansiveness of light. By viewing both paintings together, one can grasp intuitively one of the great mysteries of life: Within darkness or physical matter is light and out of that darkness comes light, love, and ever-expanding, ever-evolving life.

Biu created a sense of three dimensions and depth using directional movement and tints, tones, and shades (figure C1-2). The tints proceed from light tints in the center to deep rich tints. Behind these tints are tones and behind the tones are a few more tints, leading the viewer deeper and deeper into the folds of his design to dark shades and pure color. The way he applied the scales produced dimension, depth, and luminosity. This same composition could have been painted in a number of different ways, and each would have been different depending on how the color was applied. If you remember your design principles from chapter 1, you will recall that the way you drew your lines and the way you applied the scales can influence movement, create a sense of depth, or make the painting appear flat.

Jeff's painting represents a creative break from the radial composition (see figure C1-7). To me, Jeff's painting reflects a unique blending of his musical and visual art talents. At the center of his composition is a small circle containing the pure colors. Then he breaks away from the radial symmetry by creating an asymmetrical composition of flowing streams of light that calls to mind lines of melody. He creates an unusual balance in his composition by using tints and pure colors to create a radiation from below, counterbalanced by the shades and tones used above. In this painting you can almost hear the high notes of the tints and the low sounds of the deep tones and shades.

When Bill took my class, I called him a master of illusion because of the genius he displayed in creating his compositions. His painting, although simple in composition, was not three-dimensional until Bill added paint (see figure C1-8). The unusual thing about this painting is that you can look at it from four different directions and each direction will give you a different sense of color and light. Try turning the book to look at it four different ways. The painting works as a whole and can become a new painting by the way it is viewed, each view providing a new knowledge of color and light.

PART 3: APPLYING THE FUNDAMENTALS OF COLOR HARMONY TO PAINT

I have walked you through the mechanics of creating tints, tones, and shades, but these paintings go far beyond mere mechanics and logic of these color-mixing exercises. Each person brought his or her own energy, love, and creative consciousness to this project, thereby transcending the logical order of color. Each work is a work of art produced by artistic alchemy: the infusing of paints by the spirit or inner light. Accept this invitation to exceed your expectations by dipping deep inside yourself just as you dip your brush into your pigments.

You will now apply the fundamentals of color harmony and color mixing to creating a painting of luminescence using full-spectrum color. Here you will harness the creative powers of your imagination and intuition and the spiritual powers of inner light and love through the practice of painting.

PROJECT 1: CREATING A LINE DESIGN FOR YOUR PAINTING

MATERIALS

- Your three primary and three secondary premixed colors
- Your color wheel
- Your 9-by-12-inch tint, tone, and shade scale chart
- High-quality poster paint or designer gouache—a half-pint jar of white and a small container of jet black
- Compass
- Protractor
- 14-by-17-inch white drawing pad (any type of lightweight inexpensive drawing paper will do)
- 14-by-17-inch Bristol board pad—smooth texture, medium weight
- Pencil
- Ruler
- Scissors

- Water container
- High-quality # 6 sable watercolor brush
- Small sable # 0 and # 1 detail brushes
- Plastic mixing tray that can hold twenty or more mixed pigments or two mixing trays that can hold twelve pigments each
- Rubber cement
- Paper towels
- Small roll of masking tape
- One sheet of graphite-colored transfer paper
- Records or tapes of inspirational music

PROCEDURES

1. Take out a sheet of drawing paper, a pencil, ruler, compass, and protractor. Using your compass, make a circle that is approximately ten to twelve inches in diameter. Using your protractor, divide the circle into twelve equal sections, as you did when you made your color wheel in part 1 of this chapter. Your circle should have twelve divisions because in this project you will be using your six premixed primary and secondary colors plus the six tertiary colors you made for your first color wheel.

2. The first project is to make an interesting radial design to use as the underlying structure for your final painting. You will experiment on the drawing paper first. Choose one section from the twelve divisions and with your pencil draw various lines to create an interesting geometric pattern. You can draw free-flowing lines or you can use a ruler, compass, and protractor to create lines and shapes. Draw lines that show movement and create new shapes and spaces. Later you will paint pure colors, tints, tones, and shades within these areas. Concentrate on making an interesting design without thinking about color for the moment.

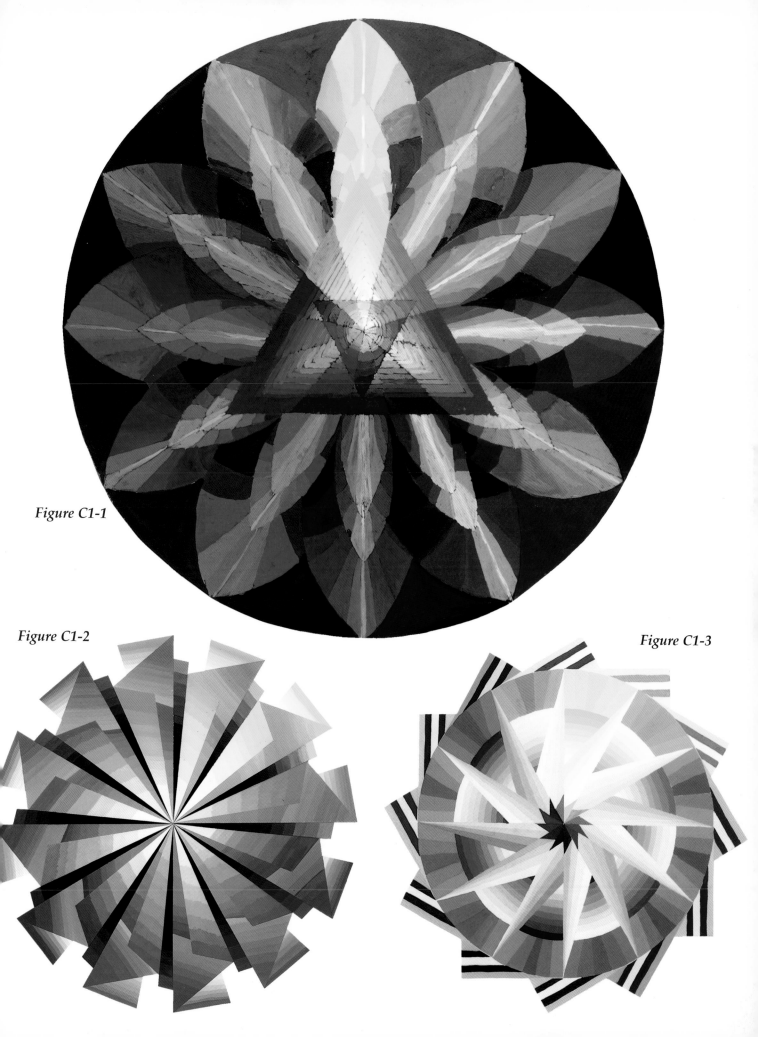

Figure C1-1

Figure C1-2

Figure C1-3

Figure C1-4

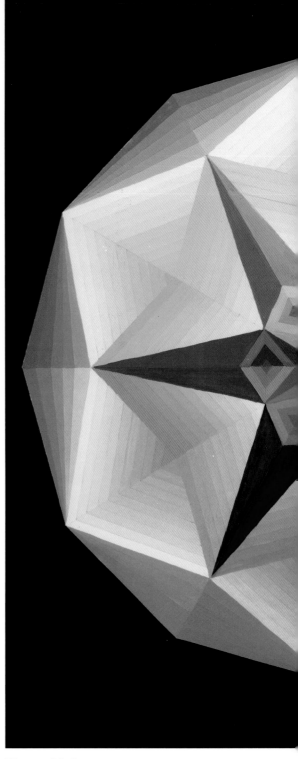

Figure C1-6

Figure C1-5

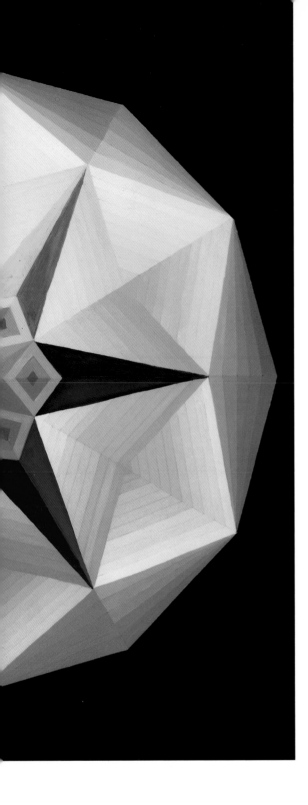

Figure C1-7

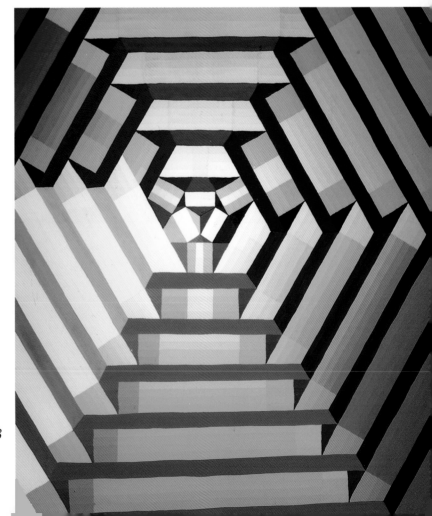

Figure C1-8

*The color and energy of light mix together
to form the imagination of the human mind.
I see the beauty and wonder of the rainbow
that glows in everyone's heart.*
—BEYOUNG

Figure C1-9

Figure C1-10

To do this gorgeous color wheel I had to look at how I felt about the flow of light and tone. I started with what I've always known—a butterfly wing, and, like a lovely song I sing, the lines and movement all did flow and the colors—how rich they glow!
 I felt great pride that I could do my best and still know there's better too
. . . more of me for another show.

—MELISSA

Figure C1-11

Figure C1-12

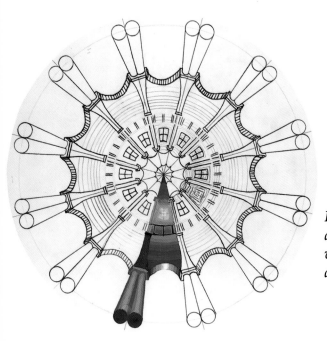

I had done some visualizations before, but they were basically undirected visualizations. Using the visualization of light, I was able to feel much more color, as well as an inner peace, an inner love. In reality what I was visualizing was my own inner self, not what I thought I should be visualizing. I wasn't visualizing . . . anything that I can read about or that anyone can teach me about. It is what I am. And you can't create that on the exterior. You have to find it on the interior. It's like touching your soul.

—Tom

Figure C1-13. *Before Tom began painting his radial design on the bristol board paper, he first experimented with tint, tone, and shade scales for one color on his drawing paper (see completed painting, figure C1-12).*

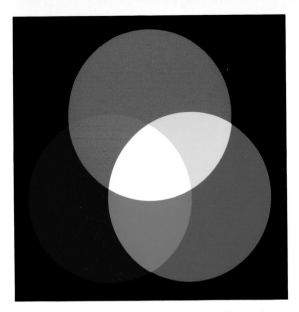

Figure C1-14. *Primary colors of visible light. The primary colors of visible light are red, green, and blue-violet. Although produced here with printers inks, this illustration serves to point out that the three primary colors of light, when mixed together, form other colors and white light.*

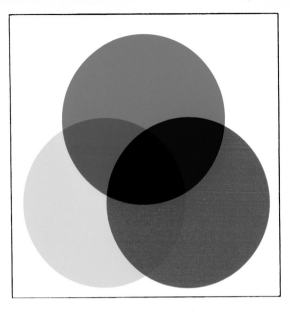

Figure C1-15. *Primary colors of pigments. This illustration shows how primary mixes of transparent printers inks—magenta, yellow, turquoise (called cyan)—create the full range of the color spectrum. To produce the color illustrations for this book, only these three colors, plus black ink, were used. You will be using these same primary colors, plus black and white, but your colors will be opaque, rather than transparent, paint pigments.*

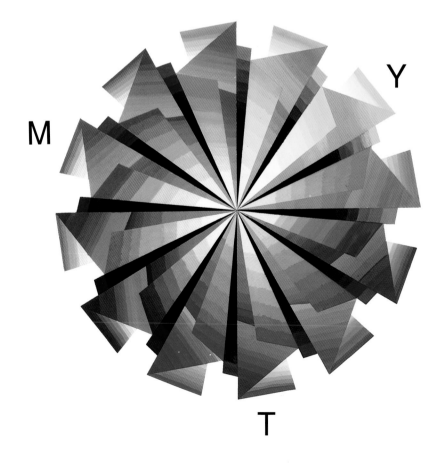

Figure C1-16. *The color wheel with twelve colors in logical spectrum order: primary colors (magenta, yellow, and turquoise), secondary colors (green, orange, and violet), and tertiary colors (red-orange, yellow-orange, yellow-green, blue-green, blue-violet, and red-violet).*

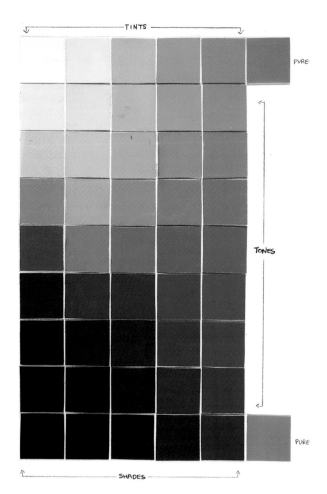
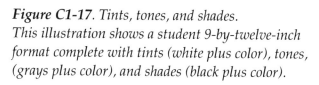

Figure C1-17. Tints, tones, and shades.
This illustration shows a student 9-by-twelve-inch
format complete with tints (white plus color), tones,
(grays plus color), and shades (black plus color).

Figure C1-18. Creating a rainbow spectrum
with paint. This illustrates the logical mixing order
for blending primary and secondary paints
to produce a variety of colors in between.

3. Before you begin, do the inner-light visualization from chapter 1 (pages 38–39) to relax you and open your creative centers. To stimulate your imagination and intuitive ability to create a radial design for your painting, do the optional guided visualization for a journey to the Golden Hall of Illumined Arts and Design in chapter 1. This time when you do the visualization, ask your inner guide for help in seeing, with the inner eye of your imagination, a line design for your painting of the color wheel. When you finish the visualization, follow the procedures as listed in chapter 1 for writing and drawing your design (page 30). Visualization will open your creativity. You may catch only a glimpse of a design or form to use, but by working with that glimpse and expanding the concept on your drawing paper, you'll find a way to develop a composition that will be uniquely yours.

4. Somewhere in your radial composition you will need to have your primary, secondary, and tertiary colors going in a logical progression (see figure C1-16). That progression may be part of the design in the center, the middle, or the outer edge. Pure colors and their logical progression can be included more than once in your final painting.

Figure 2-3. Radial design. Radial design begins from a central point and radiates outward—like spokes on a wheel. These drawings are two student examples of radial design created from a circle divided into twelve equal sections.

- Your lightest scale of light will be your tints, which can begin to radiate from the center or in some new way you have invented.

- Tones following or surrounding the tint scale of light will tend to make the tints illuminate even more brilliantly. Remember that shades are the dark scales of light, so like black, they tend to absorb color and light. Look again at the pictures here to see how others have handled the pure colors, tints, tones, and shades. These are only suggestions, however. You will find your own new and wonderful ways of expressing inner light. Here are a few points to remember when doing your initial composition on drawing paper:

- In the last chapter you discovered that your initial design did not have to be terribly complex, since complexity developed from the addition of your scale of light. Also in this design, remember that it can be simple, gaining further complexity from your innovative use of pure color, tint, tone, and shade scales.

- Review the elements of good design in part 2 of chapter 1. On your circle of twelve divisions, experiment with several designs in two or three of these divisions.

- Study the illustrations in this chapter for the underlying line/shape composition and line/scale directional movement. Note the many different positions that were used for the placement of pure colors within the paintings. Some students put the pure color in logical progressions in the center, whereas others put pure color somewhere in the middle of the composition. Others combined pure color more integrally with the scales of tones, tints, and shades.

- Notice in the illustrations that some students chose to begin shades in the center working to lighter tones and tints, whereas others chose to radiate tints in the center working into darkness.

PROJECT 2: CREATING A FULL-SPECTRUM LUMINESCENT PAINTING

PROCEDURES

1. After you have experimented with your radial line composition, select a design that you like and redraw it on a clean sheet of drawing paper. Transfer this design to a clean sheet of Bristol board paper using your graphite-colored transfer paper. Take your transfer paper and lay it face down on your Bristol paper. On top of the transfer paper, center and place your drawing, face up. Use a few pieces of masking tape to secure all three sheets of paper so that your papers do not move around while you are retracing your composition. Use your pencil to retrace your lines on the drawing paper, following the instructions outlined in chapter 1 (page 30) for retracing your black-and-white design.

2. When you are finished, set aside the design you traced on the Bristol board paper and turn to the final design you did on the drawing paper. You will now experiment with the various scales of light on this drawing. Choose one pure color from your selection of six premixed primary and secondary colors. Also have ready your black-and-white paint, water, brush, paper towels, and paint-mixing tray.

3. Before you begin put on some beautiful inspirational music. *The type of music you play while you are painting can and will influence your painting. Therefore, select only music that moves you to a higher state of consciousness and invokes in you feelings of harmony, peace, and beauty.*

4. Using the color you have chosen, fill five to ten depressions in your mixing tray with a scale of tints. They can range from almost pure white and little color to deep, richly saturated tints, mostly color with little white. In another section of your paint tray, mix anywhere from five to nine tones. Using your tint, tone, and scale chart as a guide, choose either light-, medium-, or dark-tone scales. You might consider making up several combinations, for example, one light-tone scale and one dark-tone scale. Next, mix two to four shades. Finally, fill one depression with a small amount of the pure color.

5. *Before you begin painting, sit quietly in front of your mixing tray containing all its premixed tints, tones, and shades. Close your eyes and in your mind's eye visualize the various paint mixes as pure light and energy. Open your heart and see a beam of your own inner light and love being sent to this paint mixture.*

6. You are now ready to begin painting on your drawing paper. Choose one of the twelve sections of your radial design. Decide where you will paint your pure color and paint it in that part. Next, decide where you will paint your tints, tones, and shades. *While you are painting, keep your mind focused on the image of light. It is important that you constantly think "light," not "paint," while you work.* Remember to clean your brush when you move among the various paint mixtures. When you have finished, stand back and survey this first effort. Is there a sense of luminescence in your work? See figure C1-13 for an example of Tom's original drawing paper, in which he experimented on one section of the design to make sure he was achieving radiance before going on to paint his final project.

7. If you are not satisfied with this first attempt, paint another section on your drawing, keeping in mind that you alone decide how many tints, tones, and shades to use. You also determine the direction and movement of light in your picture. If you started with the lightest scale of tints radiating from the middle, try using shades in the middle in this next section. Relax and enjoy the discovery of the many different ways you can express light using the same design and scale mixtures in your tray. Are you constantly thinking about light as you paint? If not, do the inner-light visualization again and sit quietly for a few moments filling yourself with light and love. Then go back to this experiment and, keeping inner light in your mind, begin again.

8. By the second or third section that you paint on your drawing paper, you will have decided where you will paint your tints, tones, and shades and how many of each you will need to express your sense of luminescence. You are now ready to begin painting on the Bristol board paper. You can start painting with the mixtures that you have already prepared and used for the experiment on the drawing paper.

9. Here's a helpful hint so that you do not forget the logical order of color progression: Using light pressure on your pencil, list the various colors in their right order on the outer edge of your composition. Use the color wheel you constructed for part 1 as a reference.

10. After you finish a section, clean your tray and brush well. This project becomes richer when you let yourself enjoy it without pushing to complete it, so you might think about setting aside an hour or so each day in which to complete one section of a color and its scales. As you work with each color, ask yourself how the color affects you. Does a color evoke certain emotions or memories of places, people, or events? Each color and its light is different and unique. If you find yourself staying up half the night, forgetting what time it is, or thinking about your art when you are away from it, you have hooked yourself into the creative process and the joy of creating.

11. When you mix each new color, remember from your first mixtures the number of tints you used and how light or deep in scale they were. This caution applies to the tones and shades as well. You will tune each color and its scales to the same or similar level of intensity—both for lightness and darkness—to which you tuned your first color and its scale mixtures. However, this rule is not inflexible. It applies mostly to a painting in which each section is the same repeating design, but if every other section is a different repeating design, then you might consider making different scale mixes for each.

12. When you get ready to paint with your tertiary colors, make sure you mix enough of the color ahead of time to make all the different scales you will use. Use your color wheel from part 1 as a guide to mixing your tertiary colors.

13. When you complete your painting, cut it out and glue it with rubber cement to a clean sheet of paper. Hang it up and stand back from it so you see it fresh from a distance. Acknowledge its beauty and light and realize that it is only the beginning of the many creative and beautiful ways you can express your divinity. Any time you feel you need healing energy and love, visualize this painting and its light at the top of your head, using the inner-light visualization to direct this light through you. You can also send this love and light to others.

OVERCOMING FEAR OF FAILURE

In this project you are faced with the opportunity to participate in an act of creation. If you find yourself fearful, or feel you lack commitment to finish, repeat the inner-light visualization in chapter 1 (pages 38–39). This visualization strengthens your self-love and increases your confidence in the perfection of your creative power. In doing this painting you are manifesting outwardly at a very high level the beauty, harmony, and inner light within you. You will have visual proof of your spiritual self. If the world around you seems dreary, full of pain, and anything but beautiful, be confident that the process and practice of art will enable you to see your own power to create harmony and beauty. As a consequence, you will have to stop blaming others for what is happening in your life and will need to commit yourself to developing your creative talents and to overcome your fears with love. But surely you have come this far in your artwork for just this reason.

WHAT HAVE YOU LEARNED?

Having completed both chapters 1 and 2, you have much more knowledge of how to create beauty and luminescence using ordinary paints. You have discovered more about the creative abilities of your mind and your power to focus inwardly to gain inspiration and expanded levels of consciousness. How can you continue to apply this creative ability to your everyday life?

• Look at your home environment and consider how you could change or create new color schemes that are more in tune with the beauty and light in your painting.

• If you are pursuing work or family issues that require sensitive handling, think about how you can change your mental focus and apply the power of your inner certainty to these projects.

▪ Having experienced the beauty of color using an inward focus, turn now to the outer world and look at the creations of nature. Open your eyes to the flowers, trees, birds, animals, and people. See and appreciate with new eyes the color and diversity of life around you. Most of all, appreciate who you are and that you have been given special creative power to participate in nature, to bring original beauty to nature as nature brings beauty to you.

SUGGESTED READING

Birren, Faber. *Color Perception in Art.* New York: Van Nostrand Reinhold, 1976.

Coomaraswamy, Ananda. *Christian and Oriental Philosophy of Art.* New York: Dover Publications, 1956.

Mookerjee, Ajit. *Tantra Art.* New Delhi: Ravi Kumar, 1983.

Nasar, Seyyed Hossein. *Islamic Art and Spirituality.* Albany, New York: State University of New York Press, 1987.

Roman, Sanaya. *Personal Power through Awareness.* Tiburon, California: H. J. Kramer, 1986.

NOTES

1. E. J. Brill, *The Gospel According to Thomas* (New York: Harper & Row, 1959), 19.
2. Faber Birren, *Color Perception in Art* (New York: Van Nostrand Reinhold, 1976), 38.
3. Ibid, 37.

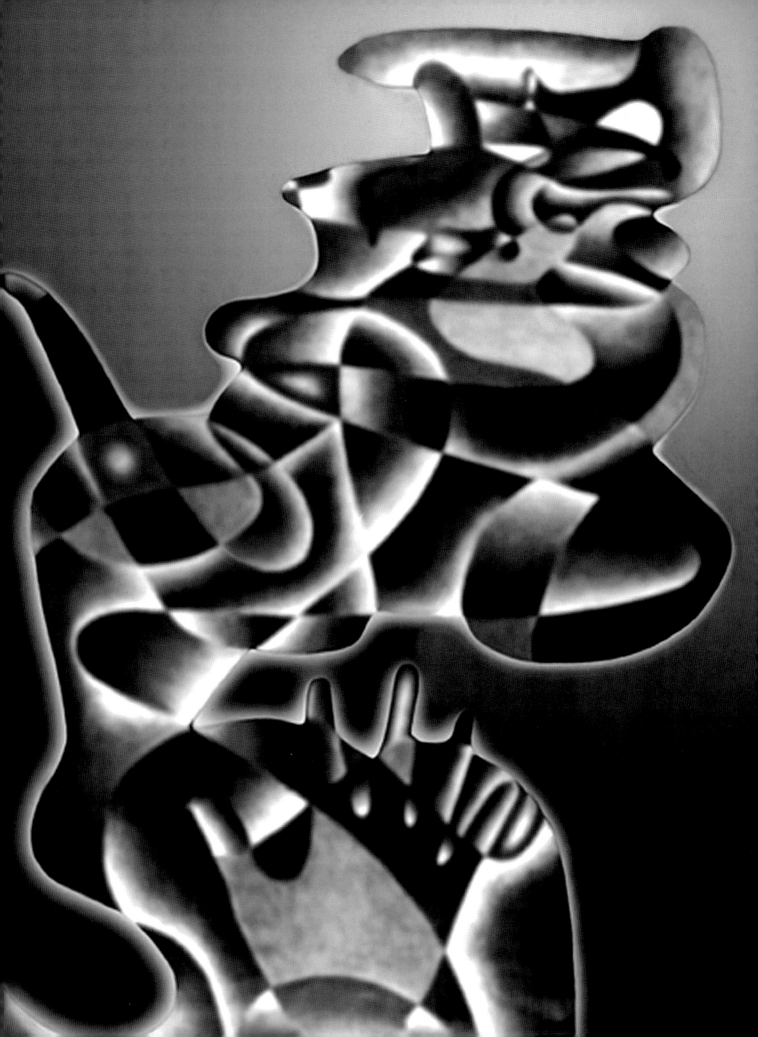

CHAPTER 3

Creative and Intuitive Drawing

A perfect path of the Truth has come into being for our journey to the other shore beyond the darkness.

—Rig Veda, 1.93.4.[1]

IN THIS CHAPTER you will work with drawing pencils to learn new ways of expressing your creativity and inner light. The beautiful and powerful examples in this chapter evolved from the first drawing assignment I give in my beginning drawing class. I'm sure you'll agree that these drawings reflect an imaginative and intuitive approach to drawing.*

The drawing projects in this chapter are not the kind given in conventional drawing classes, where students are asked to look at an object and then reproduce it on the page. Rather, these assignments encourage you to turn your attention and vision inward to create imaginative drawings using an assortment of drawing pencils. In the first project you will use a # 4B drawing pencil to achieve a smooth transitional scale of light. Next, you'll create a composition using only variations of this gradation scale, as with the light scale you created in chapter 1. In the second project, you'll make a line drawing and blend an assortment of drawing pencils to create a luminescent form. These two projects will give you the skills you need to accomplish the exciting, colorful, and imaginative project in chapter 5 using colored pencils.

Although the elements of design explored in chapters 1 and 2 apply to this drawing project as well, it will become clear that some new elements of design become important where pencil is the medium. For instance, when you mix your scale of light using pencils, you will not be adding black to white paint; rather, you will use pencils to blend a scale directly on the paper—with the white of the paper acting as your lightest value on the scale. Pencil also looks and handles quite differently from paint. Still, you'll find that pencil is quite as easy to blend and that the technical skills involved are simple to master. In this chapter, you will be building a firm foundation of drawing skills.

---

* I am deeply indebted to Fred Berensmeir, colleague and art instructor at City College of San Francisco, for sharing with me his creative teaching approach to drawing (see figures 3-6 through 3-10). The two projects in this chapter are based on his original teaching methods. I have adapted them to incorporate my use of visualizations and spiritual focus on one's inner light.

Figure 3-1. This dynamic drawing illustrates very well the use of repetition and size variation of scales. It also demonstrates major and minor movements. Movement is created visually by the way the scales are drawn. In this example the scales are fluid in movement and direction, carrying the viewer's eye in, around, and through the picture plane. The largest scale achieves a feeling of major movement as it leads the viewer's eye into other large scales. On the lower right side, small, dark scales are clustered behind the large ribbon of light, creating minor or smaller movements of light. Note that the scales behind this large movement are darker in value than the large scale. This juxtaposition of contrasting values, dark against light, or middle gradations against scales that are darker or lighter in value, creates an illusion of dimension and depth.

TAKING A NEW APPROACH TO DRAWING

Before you begin, be aware that you have almost certainly been steeped in the traditional Western approach to drawing, which stresses object orientation and a heavy focus on visible light, shadow, and external shapes. For example, in a traditional approach to drawing, you might be given a number of objects such as vases, flowers, spoons, and various other *things* to look at and draw. Or you might be told to draw the light and shadow you see on external objects (an exercise that you will do in chapter 4). The light you would focus on with your physical eyes would be external visible light. In this project, you will focus with your eye of contemplation on *inner* light and learn to become more creative. You'll create something new rather than draw an existing object. This nontraditional approach challenges your mind to be inventive. As you do these exercises, remind yourself of this shift in emphasis. If the process feels new or unfamiliar, that's because it *is* new.

Figure 3-2

The interesting thing about working this way in drawing is that you have no way of knowing for certain what something will look like until you take the risk of creating it on paper. The imaginative, intuitive approach to drawing is like life. You can act out of fear, which could immobilize you, or you can apply loving creative energies to build a better life situation. By trusting and acting on your intuition, you can safely "journey to the other shore beyond darkness" to the inner light, which when ignited will reveal the magnificent creative treasures within you.

No matter how little formal education you have had, you have an inborn intelligence enabling you to create powerful drawings like the ones you see here. Trust the creative method itself to help you to overcome fears and tap your creative potential. One of my students, Reyna, told me that by age nineteen she had had only five years of formal education. She came from South America to this country when she was a young child and her parents had kept her out of school until she was a teenager. As a result she suffered severe language difficulties and feelings of inadequacy in my class as well as in other areas of academic study. In my class, however,

Figure 3-3

Reyna learned to express her creativity nonverbally through draw-ing. She expresses her gratitude for this approach to drawing:

I used to think of art as just looking at an object and drawing it or painting it. I never saw it as a dream, something that came from your feelings or even your thoughts. Before this

Figure 3-5.This drawing is a superb example of the use of high-contrasting areas to pro-duce a sense of positive/negative space and shape. These areas are creatively balanced and inte-grated so that you can't be totally sure if the black is a shape or a space, or if the white is a shape or a space. Visually, the black and white lock to-gether, producing dramatic high contrast.

Figure 3-4. In this drawing a number of smaller scales were used to create a repetitive pattern. This amalgamation created a larger area of interest. This solution is another one for creating movement and a center of interest without resorting to use of large scales. This drawing also is a good example of visual tension. In the repetitive patterns, scales are brought close enough together to create new positive/negative shapes with the white areas.

Figure 3-6. This drawing achieves a wonderful luminous quality. The student had to think of the dark values of the pencil and light areas of the paper in terms of absorbed and reflected light. The white areas have been successfully integrated into the drawing as shapes reflecting light. This composition makes beautiful use of tonality by creating an infinite scale between pure black and pure white. Visually and psychologically, it captures a sense of multidimensional surfaces—going from flat surface to holes that drop back into deep black space filled with stars and moons.

class when I used to draw *I felt like a robot.* I did not like it. But now, just after a few weeks in this room, I've learned how to *feel, look,* and *touch* with my *eyes* . . . I have learned not to be afraid of letting myself go anymore. I'm happy because of that. Now I can think, and if I want to put my thoughts on a piece of paper, I can.

STEPPING PAST FEAR OF THE UNKNOWN

When students are confronted with a blank sheet of paper, they wonder how they can possibly create a significant drawing out of emptiness, with not even a single line to guide them. The mind doesn't want to leave the security of the known, safe waters of physical reality. Forced to plunge into the unknown wellsprings of *creative reality,* the mind often reacts fearfully and violently at first. Even professional artists face this fear at times when they begin new work. One student of mine, Rita, expresses the insecurity she felt in this situation:

A blank sheet for visual expression mocks and threatens me. Here is a barren land that I am called on to bring to growth . . . Yet as the hours of indecision force an image that is acceptable, there is a sense of relief—of satisfaction.

The process of working on your drawing will expand your imagination, overcome creative blocks, and enable you to develop trust in your intuition. So take heart! *Expect* fears to come up when half of the page is covered in images. "I'm a blank," you'll say to yourself. "I can't go on." At that point, ask yourself, "What's the worst that can happen?" The worst that can happen is that you will turn a five-cent sheet of paper totally black. Well, in that case you will have achieved a drawing of a cosmic black hole! Don't listen to the critical side of your self. That's the side that's always putting you down. Visualize your heart as being open and loving. Send a rainbow beam of love to yourself. It takes courage and creative risk to overcome fears, but these are gifts you can give to yourself.

You can do this project alone, but it is also fun to do with a number of friends. While you are working, you may find that playing of classical or meditative music is conducive to the free flow of intuition.

PART 1: LEARNING TO DRAW

The objectives of the following exercise and project are:

- To teach you how to use a # 4B drawing pencil to create a scale of light

- To apply this simple technique to the creation of an imaginative drawing

There will be no external subject matter to examine. The resource for the images and composition lies within you. Since you will make the drawing by using only tonal gradations of dark to light, the creativity in the solution lies in discovering how many imaginative ways you can apply this technique to producing an interesting composition. The scale can be thick, thin, long, wide, curved, square, or random in its course.

In this first project it is important to avoid making symbols or replicating objects from external observation. Here we are shifting away from a view of objects as separate entities to a view of an interrelated universe of energy that reflects and absorbs light. *Avoiding object orientation will help you to be more spontaneously imaginative.*

MATERIALS

- 18-by-24-inch white drawing pad
- # 4B drawing pencil
- Kneaded eraser
- Ruler
- Pencil sharpener
- Classical or inspirational music (see Appendix)

KEY CONCEPTS

If you have completed the projects in the first two chapters you will have gained a deeper understanding of the universe as vibrating energy and of your ability to use that energy in the form of paint to create original works of art. The concepts and visualizations for this project are the same as those used for the first two chapters, but they are applied to pencils. You might ask why you need to repeat the same visualizations. The visualizations used throughout this text serve very specific functions. First, they discipline and focus your mind by concentrating on inner light. Second, they are specifically aimed at developing very high levels of imagination, enabling you to reach higher levels of creativity. The mind will go in many undisciplined directions if you let it. Unless you focus your attention, you'll wind up thinking about food, what you're going to wear to a party—anything other than developing your higher creative powers.

- Fix this knowledge in your mind: The universe is composed of light and other electromagnetic energies. To do this exercise, you will visualize the pencil and white paper as atoms of pulsating energy.

- When you put a black pencil stroke on the paper, imagine that you are creating a black hole in the cosmos. The dark pencil marks, like black holes, absorb all light. Therefore, where the scale is the darkest, no light is emitted.

- The white of the paper reflects light rather than absorbs it. Visualize yourself as the conductor and choreographer, creating a dance of light scales that both absorb (black) and reflect (white) light. If you do not visualize light and energy in this way your drawing will have a tendency to be gray and washed out. *Think light! Visualize light!*

EXERCISE: HOW TO USE A # 4B DRAWING PENCIL

1. Before you can begin your drawing, you need to learn how to use your # 4B pencil to create a scale of light. Spend five or ten minutes practicing the *light scale* on a sheet of white drawing paper with your # 4B pencil, going progressively from dark to light. Start at the dark end of the scale by making heavy, smooth, black strokes. Lighten the pressure of the pencil as you proceed to the lightest end of the scale, fading into the white of the paper. The lightest end of the scale will be your white paper. Hold your pencil at an angle close to the paper in a way that allows you to move your arm, wrist, and shoulder freely. Remember that the scale of light is analogous to music: To play music you need the full scale of musical notes; to draw dynamically in this problem you need the full scale of light.

2. Don't be afraid to press hard to make your black really black. You may have to go over it a few times. Use the illustrated example as a guide. In chapter 1 you used black paint directly out of the container to get the black end of the scale, but in this project you must create pure black by learning to manipulate your pencil. Most people do not go black enough at the dark end of the scale. Don't be timid! Push yourself. See how black you can make this end of the scale. Only if you make a hole in the paper will you have pushed too deep or too hard. And since this exercise is only a warm-up for the following project a hole in the paper is no big problem.

Figure 3-7. Creating a scale using a # 4B drawing pencil. Beginning anywhere on your drawing paper, create numerous scales of light, proceeding in smooth transitions from black to white.

PROJECT 1: CREATING A DRAWING FROM YOUR IMAGINATION

PROCEDURES

1. When you have finished the warm-up exercise, take out a sheet of white 18-by-24-inch drawing paper. Using a ruler, draw a one-inch-wide border around the edge of the paper. Before proceeding further, repeat the inner-light visualization (pages 38–39). This visualization will deepen your intuition and reduce the fear that inhibits your imagination.

2. *Note:* While you are working on the drawing, it is a good idea to have an extra sheet of newsprint or drawing paper to lay over areas on which you are not working. This extra sheet is for your hands to rest on while you are working to prevent them from smudging and smearing the drawing.

3. Now you are ready to start on your drawing. Beginning anywhere inside the one-inch border you drew on the paper, create several light scales as you did on your practice sheet, proceeding from dark to light. Use your imagination and intuition to decide where to place the scales. Spend twenty minutes doing these scales. At the end of twenty minutes, stand back and look at your drawing. Did you use a full spectrum of black to white in each of the scales? Are your scales smoothly blended? If not, spend a few minutes overlapping and blending so that your eye sees a smooth transition of gradations from black to white. Is your black really black? Remember to press hard and overlap strokes to get black with no white paper showing through.

4. Now change your focus. For the next twenty minutes, see how many ways you can use the full scale imaginatively. The scale can be thick, thin, long, wide, or curved, square, or random in its course. Use the scale creatively by varying its size, shape, and direction. Avoid making symbols or objects from external reality. While you are doing this step, remember that your pencil and paper are pure energy and that you are creating a drawing of light and energy. After you have spent twenty minutes varying the sizes and shapes of the scales, stand back and look at what you have done. Can you see any empty areas on the paper that could be made more interesting by using the scale imaginatively? If so, spend a few minutes working on these areas.

5. Hang the drawing on a wall and stand back from it. As you look at it from a distance, focus on the white areas left on the paper. Look for areas of white that are beginning to take on the appearance of shapes. These shapes, created by the spaces between the pencil scales, are called *negative white spaces*. These negative white spaces can become more defined white shapes of light. Make them an integral part of the composition by concentrating your attention for twenty minutes on the white areas that look like some shape is beginning to emerge. Using the scale, tone around and away from the white areas so that the white parts take on more definite form. Stand back from your drawing and analyze what you have done. Did you miss any white areas that could be made more interesting?

6. Change your focus again. Instead of concentrating on the white areas, spend twenty minutes concentrating on the dark areas. In what areas of your drawing could you bring in more darkness? In what areas can you expand the black part of the scale to create deep black areas of light-absorbing energy? You might think about applying more black over some of the areas on which you have already drawn. Think about ways to overlap and combine smaller, less interesting areas into several larger areas—dark on dark, dark over lighter areas, and middle tones. To gain a sense of contrast and luminescence, you need to have enough darkness for the light to shine through. An analogy would be stars on a clear dark night: You can see the shimmering starlight only because most of the sky is dark.

CRITIQUING YOUR DRAWING

When you are finished, hang up your drawing and look at what you have done. If you are doing this project with friends or in a classroom, this time would be for what I call *positive critique.* Critique is, at its best, a visual analysis of a piece of artwork according to a certain set of standard criteria for good drawing and design. Critique can help you become more knowledgeable of the dynamic components of a drawing, painting, or design. It can also help you recognize areas of weakness in a composition. In this new method of drawing, these areas are ones that seem separated, isolated, or unrelated, so that the drawing lacks a sense of cohesiveness.

Until now, you have used your intuition and imagination to make creative decisions. Now it's time to use the eye of reason to analyze your composition to see if it reflects the elements of good design and creative drawing detailed on pages 96–97. You might be surprised to learn that you have intuitively satisfied a number of these criteria. If not, look for ways to subtly alter your composition.

Figure 3-8. OVERLEAF: *This drawing exhibits some of the qualities of transformative energies implied in the ancient Chinese yin/yang symbol (above). This symbol represents the dynamic interaction and balance of opposite energies. Yang is the light, active, creative male principle balanced with yin, the dark, passive and receptive female principle. This drawing demonstrates how the artist's light of consciousness (yang energy) interacts with the yin (passive and receptive energy) of pencil and paper to create whole new forms.*

Figure 3-1 (see page 81)

Figure 3-2 (see page 82)

Design Elements of Creative Drawing

• *Repetition and size variation.* Varying the size and shape of the scale helps to create rhythm and interest in your composition. If your scales are all the same size, visual monotony could result. See figures 3-1 and 3-2.

• *Visual tension.* Visual tension is created, for example, when two light scales come close together but do not touch—close enough to create a new white shape or space between them. By bringing two or more scales together so that the visual impression is one of tension between them, the white space or shape in between becomes a vital form, not just an empty white spot on the paper. See figures 3-2 and 3-5.

• *Major and minor movements.* Is there a major or large scale of light in your picture that moves the eye around and into your composition? Are there a number of small scales that create a sense of a larger form because of their close proximity? See figures 3-1, 3-4, and 3-5.

• *White as positive/negative, shape and space.* Look at the white areas of the drawing. Have you treated these white areas merely as empty spaces of white paper, unrelated to the rest of the drawing?

Figure 3-3 (see page 83)

Figure 3-4 (see page 84)

Or are the white areas integrated into the drawing as real shapes, spaces, or light? If the white areas are not visually integral to the drawing, go back into the drawing using the scale and your imagination to bring more interest to the white areas. See figures 3-3 and 3-6.

▪ *Overall harmony and interest.* Stand back from your drawing and ask yourself if the drawing is visually harmonious and interesting to you. Is there enough contrast between lights and darks? If you find that your picture gives the impression of being all middle-tone gray, then you need to add more black areas and lighten some of the gray areas. To lighten areas that are too gray or have lost some luminescence because you have smudged areas of pure white, use your kneaded eraser to clean them up. Warm the eraser in your hand and knead it like a piece of bread dough so that it is elastic. You can go back into the drawing with this eraser and remove areas that are too dark or smudged.

▪ If you sense that your drawing is still incomplete, repeat steps 4 through 7. If you are feeling fearful about proceeding and are unsure of what to do next, say aloud the positive affirmation on page 103. You can repeat these techniques as often as you need to. Think of this problem as an adventure on paper: It can never be wrong or bad, only different each time. Through intuition and imagination you can create anything you dream of.

Figure 3-5 (see page 85)

Figure 3-6 (see page 86)

PART 2: CREATING LIGHT AND FORM FROM A LINE DRAWING

The objectives of these next exercises and project are:

- To learn how to use and blend various drawing pencils
- To create an imaginary line drawing and, by blending various pencils, to change the lines into forms that radiate a sense of light and luminescence

In part 1 you used the # 4B pencil alone to produce a full scale from black to white. In this exercise you will use a full range of drawing pencils to achieve the full spectrum. When you use the pencils you will find that you can add different textures and values to the scale depending on the pencil you use.

Graphite drawing pencils come in some twenty degrees of hardness, each producing a value on the scale from black to white. I have chosen an assortment of nine pencils for this project, which will give you rich blacks and lighter values of gray. The B pencils, made of soft graphite, are coarse and grainier in texture, which makes them useful for making the black end of the scale really black. The H pencils, on the other hand, are made of hard graphite with some clay added, and are smooth in texture. H pencils are good for working the light end of the scale; they give a silky-smooth texture to the light-reflecting end.

Figure 3-9. Creating a scale using a full range of pencils. In this illustration, note that each of the pencils from # 6B through # 6H produces a scale of light. The numbers on each of the pencils stand for the value it can produce from dark to light. The # 6B is the softest and darkest; # 4B and # 2B are less soft and less black. The H pencils are harder than the Bs and are intended for the lighter end of the scale. The HB is harder in nature and lighter in value than # 2B. HB is the middle range of the scale. As the scale gets lighter each H pencil goes up in number. As this example shows, # 6H represents the lightest end of the full scale, as it is the hardest of the graphite pencils in this series.

EXERCISE 1: LEARNING TO BLEND A FULL RANGE OF DRAWING PENCILS

MATERIALS

- Two sheets of white drawing paper
- One each of drawing pencils # 6B, # 4B, # 2B, B, HB, H, # 2H, # 4H, # 6H
- Ruler
- Kneaded eraser
- Pencil sharpener

PROCEDURES

1. Take out a sheet of drawing paper and your drawing pencils. Lay out your pencils in the order as listed in the materials list. Study the illustration in figure 3-9.

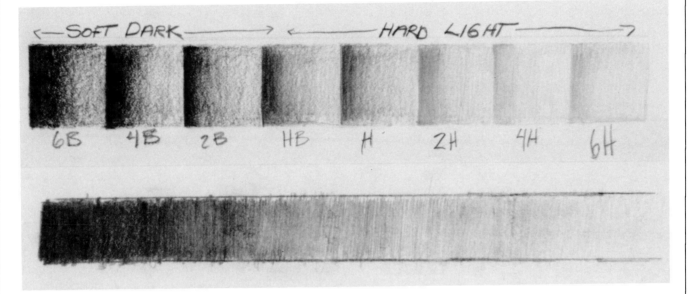

2. After you have studied the illustration, take your # 6B and on your drawing paper make a small scale just as you did for the preceding problem. Label this scale "6B." Make sure you use enough pressure to get a strong black. Next, make scales using each of the other pencils, labeling them as you go along. You will notice that by the time you get to the H pencils, no matter how hard you press you will not be able to get a black as deep as the one achieved by the soft B pencils.

3. Now line up your pencils again. This time start with the # 6B at the dark end of the scale and use each one, blending and overlapping, to create a full scale. Go smoothly and evenly from # 6B to # 6H. B pencils are the darkest (i.e., they absorb the most light). As the numbers proceed downward from 6 to 2 in the B range, the graphite becomes harder and its ability to absorb light declines. The higher the number on the H pencil, the more it reflects light, because it is harder and mixed with clay, which leaves a lighter value on the paper.

EXERCISE 2: CREATING A SENSE OF VOLUME

1. When you finish, take out a clean sheet of drawing paper and a ruler. Using the ruler and a pencil, measure and draw three 4-by-4-inch squares. Take your # 2H pencil and, using light pressure on the drawing pencil, draw a series of three or four small, medium, and large circles in each of these squares. You can overlap circles if you wish (see figure 3-10).

2. Label the first box "B pencils," the second "H pencils," and the third "B and H pencils." Go back to the first box labeled B pencils and take out your # 6B, # 4B, # 2B, and HB.

3. In your box labeled "B pencils," you will create an illusion of form by dissolving the lines of the circles. The objective of this exercise is to learn to turn lines—in this case circles—into objects that seem to have their own form, dimension, and light. Use your imagination. What you see at the moment in your box are a few lines describing circles. Before drawing, close your eyes and imagine objects that are round and full of light or reflecting light. Imagine ping-pong balls with light shining on them, or visualize eggs, planets, baseballs, or luminescent pearls. Imagine that you are holding these objects in your hand and that you can feel their solidity. *Do not begin the project until you can fully imagine one of these spherical objects.*

4. Holding this image in your mind, you are ready to begin. With your B pencils, pretend you are *sculpting a sphere* with the scale of light. Use your imagination to determine where you want the light to be, either shining on the side or top or coming from within the object. If the light is on the side or top, think about blending a darker scale around the outside of the sphere so that the lighter areas of the sphere contrast with the dark area. If you create a sphere that is dark in value, make whatever is next to it lighter in value. Using the deep, dark end of the scale next to the very light end of a scale is called *high contrast*, because the scales are far apart or opposite in value. Using a light gray value of the scale next to a middle-value gray is called *low contrast*, because the two grays are close together in value. Creating contrasts helps you to fabricate distinctions between different forms and to create illusions of depth, dimension, and light.

5. Do the same thing in the next box with the H pencils.

6. When you finish with the H pencils, proceed to the last box. In this box you will imaginatively sculpt spheres using all your H and B pencils.

Figure 3-10. This illustration shows the line drawing for figure 3-12. These simple overlapping circles were drawn freehand. Very light pencil pressure was used to make the lines. When doing your drawing, make sure that you use very light pressure—just enough to enable you to see the lines.

Figures 3-11 and 3-12. Using pencils to create form. The full range of pencils was used here to give the illusion of form and luminescence to both these illustrations. This exercise began with lightly drawn circles. Notice that you cannot see the lines anymore. The object of this exercise is to create form by dissolving *the lines.*

Although each illustration uses a full range of pencils, they are different in the quality of light that they project. Figure 3-11 is an example of low contrast in value. This low contrast creates a diffuse, pearly sense of light. Figure 3-12 exhibits a stronger contrast and bolder use of the scale. Both are beautiful and right. Your creative instincts will guide you toward your own expression of light through the use of value contrasts.

Figure 3-10

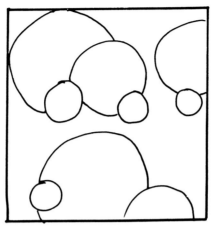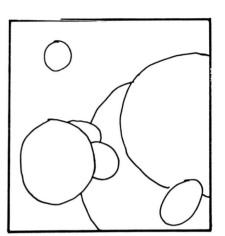

Figure 3-11

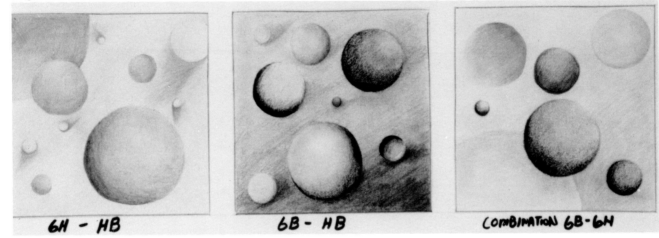

6H - HB   6B - HB   COMBINATION 6B-6H

Figure 3-12

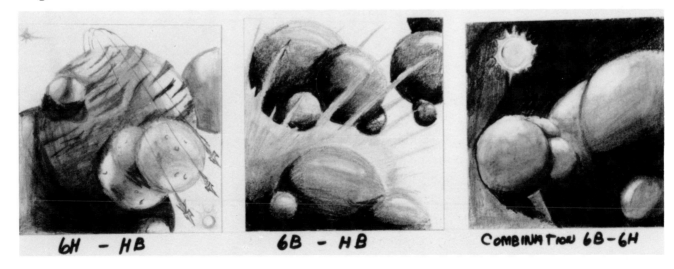

6H - HB   6B - HB   COMBINATION 6B-6H

PROJECT: CREATING A LARGE-SCALE DRAWING

This drawing will develop more fully your intuition, your imagination, and will hone the drawing skills you learned in the last two exercises. (You will need these skills in order to accomplish the project in chapter 5, which involves using and blending colored pencils.)

PROCEDURES

1. On a sheet of 18-by-24-inch drawing paper, use a ruler to draw a 2-inch-wide border around the edge of your paper. This size is only a suggested format. Before you begin your drawing, do the inner-light visualization (pages 38–39). When you finish it, repeat aloud the positive affirmation below.

MATERIALS

- See materials list for part 1.
- Play inspirational music while you work.

Positive Affirmation
Say aloud the following words:
I am wonderful!
I am great!
I am divine love and light!
I have unlimited creative potential to draw anything I can imagine!

2. Now take a minute or two to review the elements of good design (pages 32–33). Do not get too complex or too detailed in doing this line drawing. In the exercises you did with circles, you should have learned that you can easily increase complexity and add interest to a simple line drawing by using the full scale of light. The same holds true for the drawing you are about to do.

3. Now you are ready to begin. Using your # 2H pencil, *with a very light pressure,* begin drawing simple, free-flowing, overlapping lines and circles. It is important to use only enough pressure on your pencil to make your lines visible. Heavy lines are too hard to blend away. Some of the lines should touch your border. (To keep your drawing clean while you are working, lay a separate sheet of paper on top of your drawing on which to

Figure 3-13

rest your hands and to cover areas on which you are not working.) After you have completed your line drawing, take out your full range of pencils. Begin anywhere on the paper and choose one line shape to start. Use your pencils to create a sense of form and light in that shape. Continue on to other shapes. As with the exercises you did using circles, blend various pencils to create light and texture. You can also refer to these examples to aid you in making creative decisions sculpting shapes in your larger drawing.

4. Base your choice and use of pencils on the promptings of your intuition and imagination. Remember to visualize and think light while you are working. Remember to imagine solid forms before you begin. Remember to use contrasting values. And remember that the objective is to make the lines disappear by blending your scales creatively.

Figure 3-14

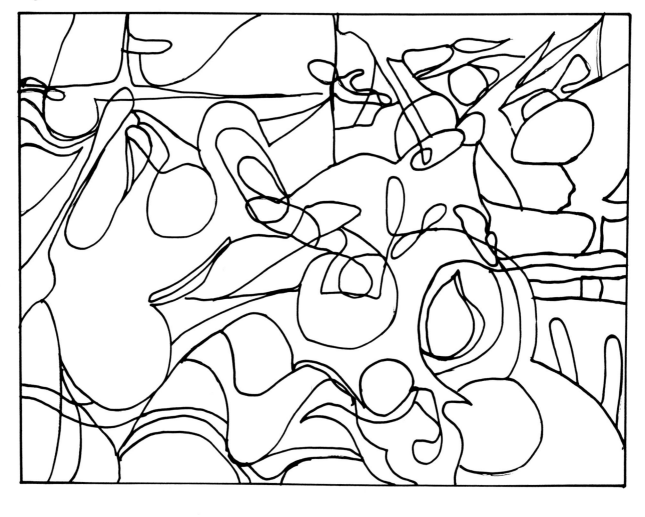

Figures 3-14 and 3-15. These two illustrations show the line drawings that were created before the value scale of light was added to create the finished drawings you see in figures 3-16 and 3-17. If you feel creatively blocked, simply draw overlapping lines without any preconceived thought and begin to experiment freely with the value scale, dissolving the lines to create form and light.

Figure 3-15

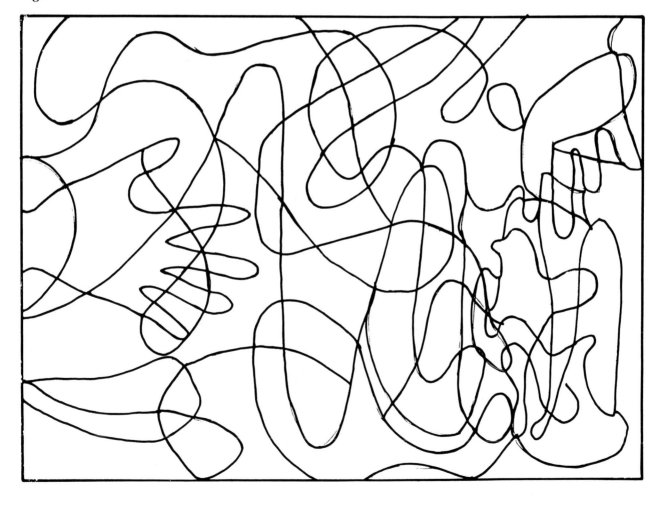

Figure 3-16. This work beautifully illustrates how new form and dimension can be wrought in a line drawing using the various drawing pencils. Note that some shapes are pure black. These black shapes, produced by the darkest B pencil, are contrasted with spherical forms lighter in value that appear to emerge behind and in front of the black. The lightest spheres radiate a smooth luster that was achieved by using and blending the H pencils. These luminescent forms contrast with forms that are darker and grainier in texture to create a sense of mystery.

Figure 3-17. Rather than emphasizing three-dimensionality, this student drawing is an exquisite example of the skillful **blending** of scales. In this drawing only a few of the shapes are pure black; several other shapes have a middle-tone value. Note that in most of the shapes a full scale from light to dark is used. In the middle of the drawing you will see that where a shape is colored darkest, the shape next to the dark edge becomes lighter in value, and where a shape ends in light, the shape next to the light begins at the dark end of the scale. This use of contrasting values, using the full scale, creates a dynamic sense of light and energy.

5. Any time you feel fearful or incapable of making a decision, hang up your drawing, look at it from a distance, and repeat aloud the positive affirmation on page 103. Open your heart to love and light. Realize that as you create your drawing you are strengthening your imagination and intuition and developing the courage to take creative risks in problem solving. The strength you develop from this creative drawing process can be applied to any area of your daily life. As you gain confidence on paper, so, too, you will gain confidence in the power of your intuition and imagination to solve everyday personal problems.

6. After you have worked on this project for about three hours, stand back from it. Hang it up and look at it from a distance. You will get a new perspective and will figure out visually and intuitively how to use the full range of pencils to create light and energy throughout the drawing. Whenever I work on a drawing or painting, I hang it up in my studio overnight so that in the morning I can see it new again. Try this yourself, arranging the drawing so that it is the first thing you see before you begin working on it. If the drawing is always lying flat in front of you, you may miss interesting developments because you will be working too close to it.

7. Study the two student illustrations and captions for this project in figures 3-16 and 3-17, but be aware that these examples are only two possibilities and solutions are almost endless. Because you are a unique individual, your drawing will be unique as well. Your drawing will reflect who you are and should not be a copy or imitation of someone else's solution.

8. When you feel that you are finished, hang up the drawing for a day or so. Change any areas that you think need to be darker or lighter. Use your kneaded eraser to lighten areas that are too dark or that are smudged. Above all, compliment yourself on your artistic accomplishment! It is easy to be critical when you have finished a work. You almost always feel that you could have done better. But these feelings, of course, are part of the creative process that challenges us continually to create from a new point of knowledge and vision. Feel good about what you have achieved in this project and let that positive energy carry you forward to face new creative challenges.

WHAT HAVE YOU LEARNED?

If you completed chapter 1 and the drawing exercises and projects in this chapter, you should be well aware of the differences between working with black-and-white paints and drawing pencils. Each medium handles differently, and each results in visual and textural differences. You used the same visualizations in both chapters and found that the basic elements of design apply to creative drawing as well as to painting. And from doing the exercises in this chapter you learned the basic skills necessary to draw. Further, you found that you need not focus on objects in the outer world to create an exciting drawing. In the first exercise, you had to trust your intuition to guide your drawing. Starting with a blank sheet of paper, you had to create something from nothing. More than likely, you experienced fear in making creative decisions because you did not even have the comfort of lines to guide you.

In part 2 you learned more about the power of your mind to fabricate imaginative forms infused with a sense of your inner light from simple line drawings. On a deeper level of understanding, you should now be more aware of the divine part of yourself. In all ancient spiritual teachings it is said that we are mortal and immortal—both human and divine. I hope that undertaking the creative challenges in this chapter led you to a deeper understanding of the divine power to create that resides within you. To become an artist—a creator—is to let yourself unfold and become more fully who you really are. To be an artist in the highest sense is to be a coparticipator in the beautiful unfolding of the universe. You can own the power of your creative nature if you believe in yourself and let go of your fears.

• List any fears you had to let go of to do these two projects. If you are working in a group, discuss your particular fears, for example, fear of failure, fear of making a decision, or fear of what others who are more "talented" might think about you. Did these fears block your creative abilities? Were you able to overcome the fears with positive affirmations, discipline, and courage?

• Think about your everyday life. Do any of the fears you listed come up when you have to make decisions at home or at work? If so, how can you apply a deep trust of your intuition to these situations? Through this creative drawing process you solved a problem by tapping your inner resources. You were the creator in charge of your drawing. Likewise, you can take responsibility for the direction and quality of your life by making decisions based on the prompting of a heart opened to love and inner light. The power of the creative process can transform not only drawing but life itself.

• Use the creative method of drawing to create pictures of how you would like your everyday world to be. On a sheet of paper, list several areas in your life that make you unhappy or that you feel need changing. Using your new drawing skills, imaginatively create on paper new positive images for your life. These images need not look like real objects. You can use abstract images to create a feeling of joy, happiness, abundance, love, and light. Meditate on your drawing while you are working, using the inner-light visualization (see pages 38–39). Visualize the essence of your images becoming a reality for you. Test for yourself the power of your own mind to manifest in your everyday world what you imagined.

SUGGESTED READING

Goldberg, Philip. *The Intuitive Edge: Understanding Intuition and Applying It in Everyday life*. Los Angeles: J. P. Tarcher, 1983.
Metzner, Ralph. *Opening to Inner Light*. Los Angeles: J. P. Tarcher, 1986.

NOTES

1. Sri Aurobindo, *The Life Divine* (Sri Aurobindo Ashram, 1977), 964.

Figure 3-18

## CHAPTER 4

Drawing Illusions of the Physical World

*A Man sets himself down with colours
and with all the Articles of Painting
he puts a Model before him & he copies that
so neat as to make it a Deception
now let any man of Sense ask himself
one Question Is this ART?*

—William Blake, Public Address[1]

Which is the art of painting designed to be—an imitation of things as they are or as they appear—of appearance or of reality? Of appearance. Then the imitator is a long way off the truth, and can do all things because he lightly touches on a small part of them, and that part an image.

THE LAST THREE chapters focused your attention inward in order to help you develop your imagination and intuition. You learned practical art skills and basic elements of design to enable you to express your inner light creatively. In this chapter you will completely change your focus from the inner world to the outer world. The chapter presents two projects calling for the drawing skills you learned in chapter 3. In part 1 you will learn how to draw in three-dimensional perspective and how to create illusions of visible light and shadows on a sheet of paper. In part 2 you will set up an arrangement of boxes or bones and focus on drawing the light and shadows that fall on these objects. The point of these exercises is to give you practice in switching from the functions of imagination and intuition to the cognitive functions of logic, reason, and visual perception through the physical eyes. You will train your mind, eyes, and hand to work in harmony to produce images that you see in the external world.

INTEGRATING YOUR THREE "EYES" OF VISION

This outward focus is based on the traditional drawing skills discussed in chapter 3—the skills that allow you to render spaces, shapes, visible light, and shadows. These methods will heighten your awareness of the richness of the external world and will round out your tool box of drawing techniques. By practicing these skills you will be able to combine the kinds of knowledge you possess:

- Knowledge gained through your inner light by seeing intuitively and imaginatively through the eye of contemplation
- Knowledge gained through intellectual light by seeing through the eye of reason
- Knowledge gained via visible light by seeing through the physical eyes

ART AND IMITATIVE ART

If you are like most students in my drawing classes, you can't wait to learn how to draw a picture that looks like something you have seen—a house, a person, or a landscape. You might regard any ability you have in this direction as a sign that you have artistic talent. But think a moment. Would your ability to draw *exactly* what you saw really be a sign of artistic ability? At the beginning of this chapter are two quotes, one from the Greek philosopher Plato, fourth century B.C.; and one by William Blake, genius, artist, poet, and prophet of eighteenth-century England. Both Plato and Blake believed the physical world to be deceptive and only a part of a much greater spiritual reality. Their profound understanding of the real creative potentials within humankind made them critical of artists who merely copied what they saw.

Blake studied art for a short time at the Royal Academy of Art in England. He encouraged artists to learn the skills of drawing by observing and drawing from the human figure and other forms of physical reality. He was in no way opposed to developing one's drawing abilities by observing and drawing physical objects, but he used this type of drawing only as a point of departure for his creative work: the imaginative expression of his inner visions. You will find an analogy in the work you will do in the next chapter, when you will use reference material from books and magazines to flesh out images from within.

Before you begin the first project, study the student examples to gain a clearer understanding of the distinctions between what Blake and Plato called art and imitative art. Figure 4-1 is a very good example of the work you are about to do: drawing a corner of a room and rendering the light and shadows. One of my students, Dawn, made this drawing after only three months of training in my beginning drawing class. This example would be considered very accomplished for a beginner by most traditional standards of Western art practice. But is it art? Both Plato and Blake would say no. Why? Because the drawing only imitates the appearance of a room—a room that someone other than the artist already created. To do this drawing, Dawn needed only to observe carefully and draw what she saw: spaces, shapes, light, and shadow. She did not need to use her imagination, intuition, or inner light to make this drawing.

Figure 4-1.
Drawing of room.

Now study figure 4-2. Dawn also did this drawing, and it was her very first drawing of the same semester. Figure 4-2 is Dawn's solution to part 1 in chapter 3. It shows great creativity and demonstrates more clearly than the other drawing Dawn's real potential for original artistry—manifested from *inside* herself. Here Dawn had to use the problem-solving abilities of her imagination and intuition in order to express herself creatively. After a semester in beginning drawing, Dawn says:

> I've learned that talent has nothing to do with art. It goes much deeper than that. Art is about being human, and we are all artists.

As you do the following exercises, be aware that by focusing outwardly you will be using only a small portion of your brain and none of your higher creative faculties. As you do this project, keep in mind an understanding of the *type* of knowledge you are gaining through your physical sense of sight.

Figure 4-2. Creative intuitive drawing.

PART 1: DRAWING ILLUSIONARY LIGHT, SHADOWS AND PERSPECTIVE

PROJECT 1: PERSPECTIVE LINE DRAWING OF A ROOM

There are two main ways to create an illusion of depth on a flat piece of paper: mechanical perspective and sighting perspective. *Mechanical perspective* was originally developed by the artists of the Renaissance and is based on a set of analytical principles called one-, two-, and three-point perspective. This type of perspective is

Figure 4-3

Figure 4-4

used mostly by architects, engineers, and product designers, although a number of artists also employ it. *Sighting perspective*—the kind you will learn in this project—is based on external observation. You will learn to suspend your analytical functions of logic and reason and switch to a spatial function of the brain that identifies shapes and space. Quite simply, in order to do sighting perspective, you will need to train yourself—and coordinate your mind, eyes, and hands—to *see* and *draw* the shadows, light, angles, and lines of outer-world phenomena without analyzing or naming the objects you are drawing. This exercise will sharpen your ability to observe the dynamic interconnections of outer reality as presented to your physical eyes.

Figure 4-5

Figure 4-6

In the last chapter you drew a format or rectangular frame for your pictures. You'll draw a frame here, too, but you'll also have a smaller version of the frame to hold in your hand and look through while you are drawing. The hand-held frame will help you focus selectively on the area of the room that you will be drawing, just as the viewfinder of a camera allows you to focus on a subject. Whatever you see through this *focusing frame,* you will draw— though in larger scale—in the rectangular format you drew on your paper. If you are like most students I have taught, you will

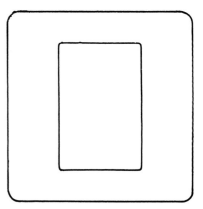

Figure 4-7. *Line drawing of a focusing frame.*

Constructing a Focusing Frame

PROCEDURES

1. Take out your scissors, transfer paper, ruler, pencil, tracing paper, masking tape, and a small piece of heavy paper or Bristol board (paper that stays firm when you hold it up). Lay your tracing paper on top of the illustration in figure 4-7 and secure it with a small piece of tape. With your pencil and ruler, copy the illustration precisely.

2. Next, put the heavy piece of paper in front of you and lay a small piece of transfer paper face down on top of it. Put your tracing paper face up on the transfer paper. Secure all three pieces so that they do not move. With a ruler and pencil, using medium pressure, trace over the lines you draw on the tracing paper.

3. When you finish, remove the tracing and transfer papers from your heavy paper. With your scissors, carefully cut out the center rectangle to make a small rectangular window. Your focusing frame is ready and you can begin.

MATERIALS

- Scissors
- Masking tape
- Transfer paper
- Ruler
- Pencil
- Small piece of heavy paper —like bristol board

find that you have not really learned to see or observe outer phenomena accurately and that your eyes are completely undisciplined in this regard. The hand-held focusing frame will discipline your eyes so you can concentrate on a specific area. You'll wind up seeing outer-world phenomena in startling new ways.

Before you begin to draw, you will need your focusing frame. You can use an empty 35mm slide holder or you can construct a frame out of paper by following the instructions in the accompanying box. The 35mm slide holder works well because it is easily available, easy to use, and works for the following rectangular formats: 18 by 24 inches, 12 by 16 inches, or 9 by 12 inches. Therefore, whatever I see in the slide holder and draw in any of the above format sizes will be in proportion in the larger scale.

MATERIALS

- White drawing paper: 18 by 24 inches, 12 by 16 inches, or 9 by 12 inches
- # 4B drawing pencil
- Kneaded eraser
- Ruler
- Empty 35mm slide holder or a frame made in accordance with the section called Constructing a Focusing Frame
- Inspirational music

PROCEDURES

1. Take out your ruler, a white sheet of drawing paper, your # 4B drawing pencil, a kneaded eraser, and an empty 35mm slide holder or a frame you have constructed. On your drawing paper, using your ruler and pencil, draw a 9-by-12-inch rectangle.

2. Holding your small focusing frame in a vertical position, look through it and select a corner of a room you want to draw. As you look through the frame, move it back and forth. Notice that the perspective changes. Move the frame around until you see a corner in an interesting perspective from which to draw.

3. Now you are ready to draw. Place your drawing paper in a vertical position in front of you. The 9-by-12-inch rectangle on your drawing paper is analogous to your smaller focusing frame. Whatever you see through the small rectangular window, you will draw proportionally to a larger scale inside your 9-by-12-inch rectangle. Think of the image in your focusing frame as a miniature version of the drawing you will do inside the larger rectangle on your paper. For example, you will draw any lines you see touching the edges of your focusing frame in the same relative position on your 9-by-12-inch rectangle.

4. Before you begin to draw, focus your small frame on the corner of the room so you can see part of the ceiling where the two corners of the room and part of the floor meet. Make sure that both your paper and the focusing frame are in a *vertical* position. I have seen students struggling to draw with their paper in a horizontal position while holding the focusing frame in a vertical position, so check before you begin.

5. Once you have chosen your subject, you will retain it throughout the exercise, just as you hold the camera steady once you have focused on a picture. As you begin to draw, you will find yourself looking back and forth from the framed view to your drawing. If you relax the hand that is holding the frame while drawing, remember to put the frame back in the same position each time you look through it. Also, try closing one eye while looking through your focusing frame.

6. In the second drawing project in chapter 3, you created an imaginary line drawing before you added your scale of light. In this exercise you will also start with a line drawing first. But this time you will draw the lines of the room as you see them, not as you think they should be or as you imagine them to be.

7. Look through your frame and notice the angle at the top of the ceiling that is formed by the two walls coming together. Draw that shape, making sure the angle lines are connected to the edges of your drawing paper format in the same position and at the same location as in your focusing window. Next, draw the angle you see where the two walls come together on the floor. Again, make sure the lines touch the edges of the large format in the same places as in the frame.

8. Starting at the point on the angle where the two walls of the room meet in the top corner, draw a vertical line straight from this point until you reach the point of the angle of the floor. Make sure your vertical line is parallel to the vertical edges of your rectangle. You can use a ruler as a guide or you can draw the line freehand. If your vertical line is parallel to your edges but does not meet the point on the floor angle, then you know you have drawn one of your angles wrong. Look again, and draw the angle once more. You now have established your ceiling, two walls, and the floor.

9. At this point, draw all the vertical lines you see in your frame. Measure lengths and distances not mathematically but proportionally, as they relate to the scale of your whole composition.

10. Next, draw all the other lines and shapes you see. Think not in terms of objects but in terms of space, shapes, angles, and vertical and horizontal line connections.

11. Check lines that look like they are horizontal. If they are truly horizontal they will be parallel to the top or bottom edge of your format. You can check by holding your pencil perfectly horizontally in front of your focusing frame. If you find the lines are not parallel to the top or bottom edge of your frame, then draw them at the angle you see them. See the corner as a large rectangular composition composed of interconnecting lines and shapes.

12. *Do not think—but draw exactly what you see.* If you find you are fighting with the function of your brain that is being critical of this procedure, tell it to be quiet. Say aloud the following affirmation: *Left brain, be quiet! This is not a job for you to do. I fully possess the talent to draw what I see.*

CONFLICT AND SENSE OF DUALITY

In split-brain studies, researchers have found that in some patients with severed corpus callosum—the tissue that normally connects the two hemispheres of the brain—it seems almost as if a different personality resides in each half of the brain and that the two identities seem to struggle against each other. I have actually witnessed a similar struggle in some of my students. Certain tasks call this dual-brain battle into action by permitting two different kinds of approaches: logical and purely perceptual.

This battle shows up most clearly in sighting perspective projects. For example, one student, a computer science major, was taking my drawing class for extra credit. When it came time to do this project, she told me she was having an internal battle. She remembered that I had told her to draw *exactly* what she saw in front of her, but an inner voice refused, arguing that the drawing she was about to make was not *logical* and that the way she wanted to render a building was all wrong. In the end she gave in to the critical voice and made a drawing that failed to capture the perspective she was after.

If you find such a battle occurring within yourself, repeat the positive affirmation above as many times as you need to. Tell the left brain to be quiet! Even if your left brain is not causing the problem, being firm with it will help you turn off your logical, critical half.

PROJECT 2: DRAWING ILLUSIONS OF SHADOWS

PROCEDURES

1. When you have finished, you should have a line drawing of the corner of your room (see figure 4-8). Stand back from the drawing and check to see if your angles and lines are correct. If they are not, use the focusing frame to check your shapes and lines. Make any corrections you need to make.

Figure 4-8. Before adding shadows to your drawing, make a simple sighting-perspective line drawing of your room.

2. Once you have drawn the corner of your room, go back to the same corner at nighttime. Turn on a lamp and set it on a table or on the floor. Direct it so that the light casts deep shadows onto the surfaces of the room.

3. Using your frame, focus on the same area. This time, look at the deep shadows that are cast on the wall and surrounding areas. Concentrate on the shapes of the shadows. With your pencil, using very little pressure, outline the shapes of the shadows on your original drawing. Shadows do not have harsh outlines but are soft; they blend into and follow the contour and shape of the environment. You will use your # 4B pencil to blend these shadows onto your original drawing.

4. Before you begin, notice that not all the shadows have the same value: Some are dark and some are light. Some have a full range of values evolving from dark to light. When you are blending your shadows, pay attention to the darkness or lightness of the shadows and scale them accordingly. As an aid for figuring out your values, refer to the pencil light scales you made for exercises in chapter 3.

5. When you have completed your drawing, use your kneaded eraser to remove areas that are smudged or that need to be lightened.

WHAT HAVE YOU LEARNED?

Before you go to the next project, reflect on what you have learned in this exercise. Answer the following questions:

- What new skills did you learn by doing this project?

- Were the new skills you learned drawing skills, visual skills, or a combination of both?

- By doing this project, were you able to tell the difference between your analytical abilities (logic and reason) and your visual abilities to see spaces, shapes, light, and shadow?

- Do you *see* the corner of your room differently as a result of this exercise?

- In this exercise you focused the light of a lamp to create deep contrast between light and shadows in the room. Is this light the same kind you visualized in order to do the projects in the previous chapters?

- Compare the drawings you did in the previous chapters with the drawing you just did. Which do you feel developed your creativity the most? The least? Why?

- Would you agree or disagree with Blake and Plato when they said that merely copying an object is imitative and uncreative art? Bring up this question with friends who have an interest in art.

PART 2: DRAWING VISIBLE LIGHT AND SHADOWS

Every sort of confusion is revealed within us; and this is that weakness of the human mind on which the art of conjuring and of deceiving by light and shadow and other ingenious devices imposes, having an effect upon us like magic. *The prison den is the world of sight.* [italics added]

—PLATO, *The Republic VII, X*[3]

For centuries humankind has looked in awe at the physical world, charmed by the beauty of its light and shadows. The work illustrated here is alluring, powerful, and magical. To do this exercise, my beginning drawing students sat in a darkened room around a still life of animal bones that were painted white. The only lights in

Figure 4-9

Figure 4-10

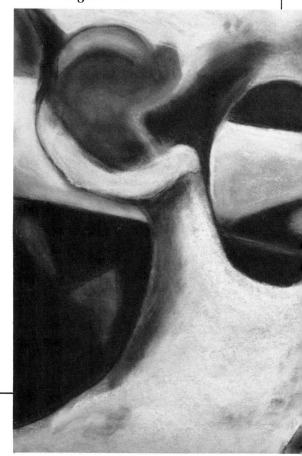

the room were spotlights focused on the bones to create a strong contrast of light and shadow. Using white pastel chalk and charcoal, the students concentrated on drawing spaces, shapes, light, and shadows. These pictures were done by different people drawing from the same still life, yet each gives a totally different picture and perspective. Each person came up with a unique, dynamic composition of light and shadow.

The following projects will further strengthen your abilities to discern and draw visible light and shadows. You will use new drawing materials here—charcoal and white pastel chalk—and will learn how to use the focusing frame to exaggerate your subject matter so you can create a truly dynamic composition. You will discover that there are many ways of perceiving the same object and that physical appearances change as a result of light, shadows, and your own personal perceptions and perspective.

Figure 4-11

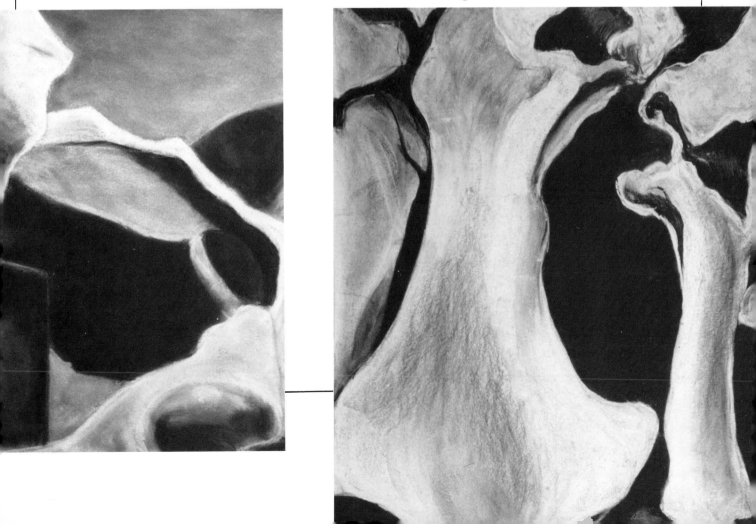

The projects are designed for group participation, but if you are doing them alone you will draw the still life you set up from two or more positions. By doing two or more drawings from different perspectives, you increase your awareness of the illusionary nature of light and shadows. You will need the materials listed below for each of the following projects.

MATERIALS

- Two sheets of middle-tone gray pastel or middle-tone gray cover stock paper (middle-tone gray is the middle color on your scale of light, between black and white)
- One sheet of newsprint or drawing paper
- One stick of white pastel chalk
- One stick (round or square) of soft compressed charcoal
- One stick of soft vine charcoal
- Kneaded eraser
- Ruler
- Pencil
- Soft cloth or rolled paper tortillion (also called a charcoal stump) for blending
- Your focusing frame
- Various shapes and sizes of animal bones that have been painted white (If you have difficulty finding animal bones for your still life, use various sizes of cardboard boxes that have been wrapped in white paper or that have been sprayed or painted white.)
- Large black or dark-colored cloth or a large black sheet of paper
- Two or three clip-on spotlights
- One can of spray fixative
- Inspirational music

Figure 4-12

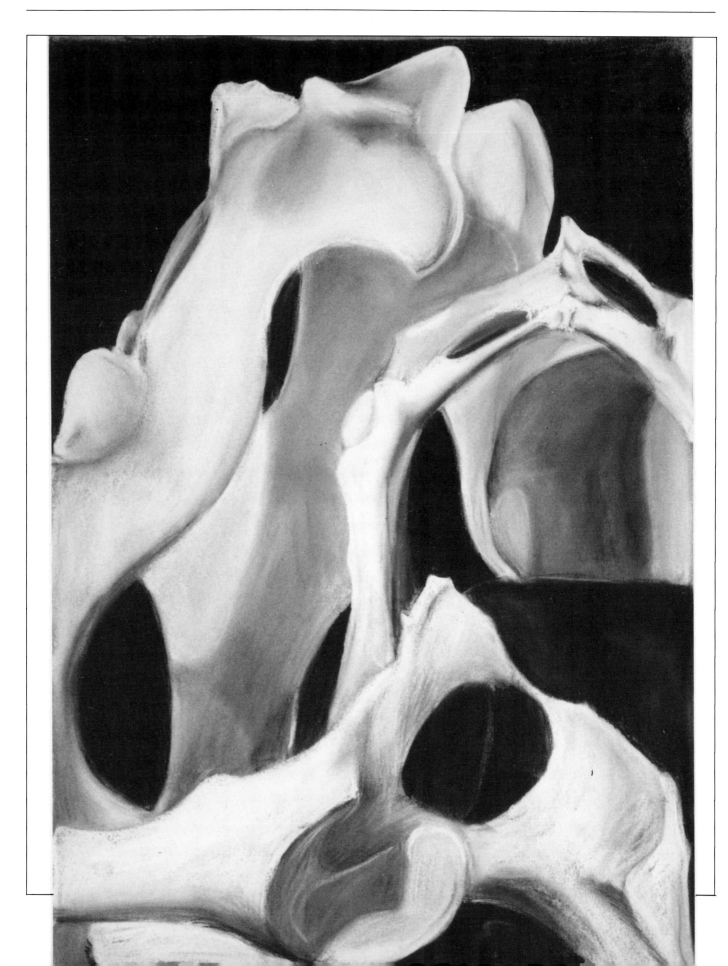

PROJECT 1: DRAWING A STILL LIFE

The first step is setting up your still life. If you do not have a room that can be darkened during the day, you will need to do this project at night. Place a table in the middle of the room and cover it with the black cloth. Arrange your bones or boxes in the middle of the table so that the arrangement looks interesting from a number of different points in the room. Arrange your objects so that you can see spaces between some of them. These spaces should look like interesting shapes (an applied element of basic design in which spaces can be seen as either positive or negative). Next, place your clip-on spotlights in two or three different places in the room, near the still life and high above it. Turn on the spotlights and turn off all other lights. Focus the spots so that you create high contrasts of light and shadows on the objects.

PROCEDURES

1. Take out one sheet of gray paper and your pencil, ruler, focusing frame, and white pastel chalk. Using a ruler and pencil, measure and draw a 12-by-16-inch rectangle on your gray paper.

2. In this exercise you can choose to make either a vertical or horizontal drawing. Be sure to hold your focusing frame in the same position as your paper.

3. Use your frame to focus on a portion of the still life so that parts of the still life touch at least three sides of your frame. The point is not to capture a whole view of the still life but to move in and focus on part of the still life so that it appears larger than life and becomes almost an abstract image. By focusing this way, you automatically exaggerate the size of the bones. Exaggerating your subject matter will help you to see the bones not as objects but as shapes of light and shadow, which will enable you to create a very dynamic composition.

4. Remember, do not change the position of your focus once you have decided on an area to draw. Always hold the frame in the same position when you are drawing.

Figure 4-13

5. Before you begin drawing, look through your frame and focus on just the spaces around and between the bones. See these spaces as shapes. With your white pastel chalk, lightly draw the outline of the spaces onto your paper in the same relative position that they occupy in your frame.

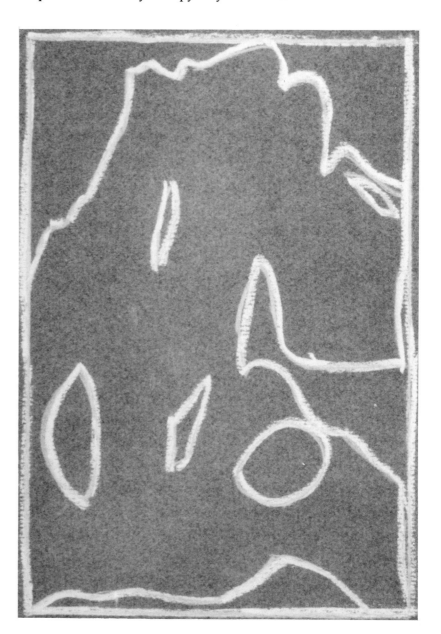

Figure 4-14. This illustration shows the line drawing for spaces around the bones. By drawing the spaces around your still life first, you automatically define the outline of your objects.

6. Next, look through your frame and focus on the bones. See them as silhouette shapes. On your drawing paper, using light pressure on your white chalk, draw just the outlines of these shapes. The result will be a white line drawing of spaces and shapes.

Figure 4-15. After you have drawn the shapes of your spaces, you will find it easy to draw the outer edge, or silhouette, of your objects. Doing this creates an interconnecting line drawing on your paper, giving you a basic structure and point of reference from which to work.

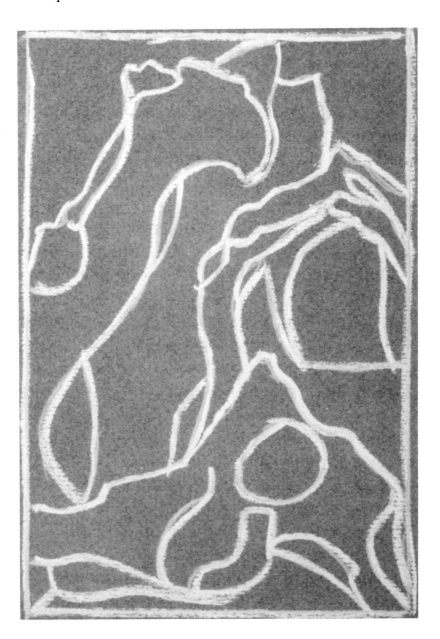

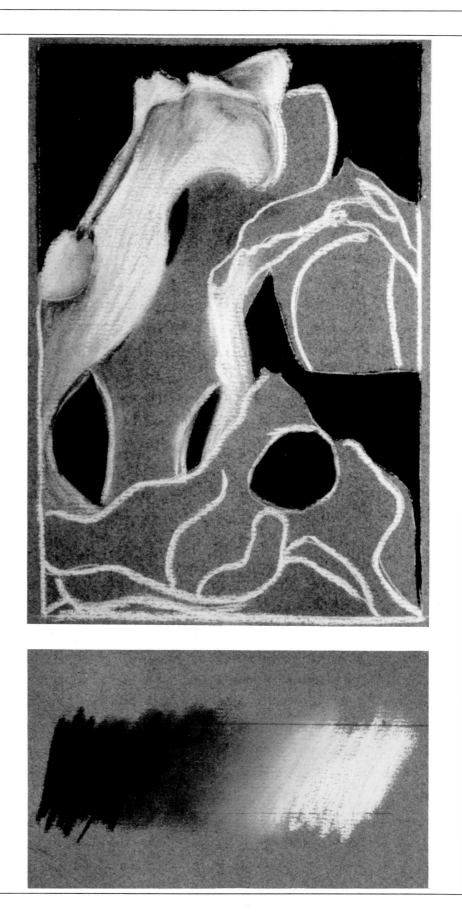

Figure 4-16. *Having completed the first two steps, it is now time to create a sense of volume and light using your chalk and charcoal. Make a scale of light on a strip of your gray paper, considering the gray of the paper to be the middle of your scale of light. I find it easiest to start with the darkest and lightest values first. Use your compressed charcoal to darken any area that is black. For the light or whitest area, use your white chalk. For the subtle in-between areas, use your stump to blend the various charcoals and white chalk.*

PROJECT 2: CREATING ILLUSIONS OF LIGHT AND SHADOW USING CHALK AND CHARCOAL

PROCEDURES

1. Take out your second sheet of gray paper. Once you have made your line drawing, you will spend the rest of the time drawing the light and shadows you see. Think of your gray paper as the middle tone of the light scale. The middle tone of light is already present in the paper. Do not think of the paper in terms of gray. Think of it as light or energy that both reflects and absorbs—a blend of both black and white. Imagine your white pastel chalk as the light end of your scale. Imagine the compressed charcoal as the black end of your scale. Soft compressed charcoal is dense and will give you a nice range of color from black to middle-tone values on the scale. Your vine charcoal stick is less dense and will produce middle tones to light tones on your scale. You will find charcoal and chalk quite easy to use and blend, somewhat like using powdered paints on paper. But instead of mixing the media in containers, you will mix and blend the charcoal and white chalk directly on your paper to achieve the full scale of light going from black to white. Because you are using a middle-tone gray paper, you need only blend your materials from the darkest to the lightest, leaving any middle-tone values you see as the gray of your paper. On your second sheet of paper, experiment blending a full scale of light. Start with the compressed charcoal as the darkest value, proceeding with vine charcoal mixed with white chalk to create a smooth blend from dark to light.

2. Take out a sheet of newsprint or drawing paper and your charcoal sticks, kneaded eraser, and soft cloth for blending. Before you begin, sit quietly in front of the still life with your drawing materials and visualize the materials and the still life as being composed of pulsating atoms of light and energy.

3. Next, look through your focusing frame and concentrate on the shadows and light you see falling on the still life. See the shadows and light as shapes. You will use the white pastel chalk to draw the lightest shapes and the charcoal sticks to draw the darker shadow shapes. Use your newsprint paper to cover areas of your drawing on which you are not working. (These powdery materials tend to smudge easily.)

4. Concentrate now on seeing only the lightest or brightest shapes of light. Using your white chalk, blend these shapes onto your paper. Next, focus on the darkest shadows until you see them as shapes. Using your charcoal sticks, blend these shapes onto your paper, remembering that the compressed charcoal is for the darkest and deepest shadows and the vine charcoal is for the gray areas of shadow and light.

5. As your eyes become more accustomed to looking at light and shadows, look for subtle degrees of shadow and light. Avoid drawing shadows and light as harsh, hard-edge shapes. Shadows blend and bend into one another. Use your finger, the soft cloth, or rolled paper tortillion to blend smooth transitions. You can also use your kneaded eraser to lighten areas.

6. When you feel you have finished, stand back and observe what you have done. Have you gone far enough into the black part of the scale? Have you used enough pure white? Have you used the full range of light, from very dark to very light? If not, go back into the drawing and rework. Have you toned your shadows so that the transitions are smooth and blend into one another?

7. For those spaces and shapes that you consider background in your drawing, you might want to use your compressed charcoal to make them a deep, dark shape or space. These dark areas can add high contrast and will highlight the subtle gradations of the middle- to light-value areas of your drawing.

8. When you are finished, use your kneaded eraser to clean up areas of the drawing that are smudged. Then take your can of spray fixative and spray a light coat on top of your drawing to protect it from further smudging.

WHAT HAVE YOU LEARNED?

THE ILLUSIONARY NATURE OF PHYSICAL REALITY

By the time you finished this project, you probably were no longer sure what defined the reality of what you drew. Was it the spaces, the shapes, the light and shadows, or the objects themselves? You focused your attention on drawing light and shadows, yet the end result was the image of bones on your paper. If you drew the still life from several points of view or did this project with a group, you found that no one drawing was the same, and that no matter how many times you drew it, or how many people drew it, you could not capture an identical and complete image of what was in front of you.

In doing this drawing, you may have become more aware of the illusionary nature of ordinary reality and the many ways you can perceive an object. Perhaps before you did the exercises in this book you tended to view the outer world as separate from yourself, since you relied primarily on external sensory input, symbols, analytical logic, and reasoning as ways of gaining knowledge. You probably made judgments about yourself, other people, art, science, and everyday events based on this type of perspective.

Using this drawing exercise as an illustration of deeper truth, realize that your perspective is colored only in part by personal beliefs, culture, logic, and sensory perception. By doing the projects in this book, I hope you have learned that your inner knowledge and vision combine with logic and sensory perception to provide a picture that integrates your spirit with the world outside and unleashes your full creative capacity.

Based on your experience of doing this drawing exercise, answer the following questions:

- How has this exercise strengthened your drawing skills and ability to perceive visible light and shadows?

- What defines outer reality: light and shadow, spaces and shapes, or objects? Using this process of observation (seeing with the physical eyes), were you able to know the whole truth about the object you drew?

- Take the preceding question one step further. Using this type of perception alone, can you know the whole truth about a person or other sensory events?

- How does this project, which has an outward focus on light, differ from the projects you did with an inner focus on light? Is outer light the same for you as inner light?

- Which of the two kinds of projects that you've done elicited more creativity from you—those that focused on external or internal reality?

- Have you found that doing these exercises has changed your way of looking at the world?

As you work on the exercises in these chapters, you may find that you are beginning to see the world with new eyes—an integration of your three "eyes" of vision. With new eyes and an open heart and mind, begin to appreciate the creative power within you. Realize that your knowledge and vision, of both inner and outer truths, enrich your awareness of the world. Begin to appreciate and respect the differences you find in other people, and go beyond the illusion of appearances to appreciate the magnificence within you and all people. With love in your heart, acknowledge the light inside of you. Realize that you have creative power over your own destiny and that the quality of your life is based on how you perceive your reality, how you choose to focus your mind, and how you use the creative materials of this world to express yourself.

SUGGESTED READING

Edwards, Betty. *Drawing on the Right Side of the Brain*. Los Angeles: J. P. Tarcher, 1979.

Erdman, David V. *The Poetry and Prose of William Blake*. New York: Doubleday, 1982.

Frank, Frederick. *The Zen of Seeing: Seeing/Drawing as Meditation*. New York: Vintage, 1973.

Harmon, Willis. *Global Mind Change*. Indianapolis: Knowledge Systems, Inc., 1988.

Nicolades. *The Natural Way to Draw*. Boston: Houghton Mifflin, 1941.

Plato. *The Republic*, Books VII and X.

Schorer, Mark. *William Blake: The Politics of Vision*. New York: Vintage, 1959.

NOTES

1. David V. Erdman, *The Poetry and Prose of William Blake* (New York: Doubleday, 1982), 566.
2. Plato, *The Republic*, Books VII and X
3. Ibid.

CHAPTER 5

Visions of a Peaceful Planet

I was standing on the highest hill in the center of the world. There was no sun, but so clear was the light that what was far was near. The circle of the world was a great hoop with two roads crossing where I stood, the black one and the red. And all around the hoop more people than I could count were sitting together in a sacred manner.

—Eagle Voice (a Lakota holy man)[1]

THE BEAUTY AND serenity of the pictures in this chapter (see color insert, figures C2-1 through C2-12) reflect the spirit of a peaceful planet. These images have a remarkable power to touch the heart and take the viewer to a deeper level of appreciation for the magnificence of a living earth.

It may be difficult for you to believe, but these drawings, with their highly sophisticated and unique use of color, were made by students in beginning drawing class after doing the two drawing projects outlined in chapter 3. The exercises and project in this chapter build directly on the drawing skills you learned in chapter 3. Here, too, you will create beautiful images by going inward, through the process of a special guided visualization. The images you receive as a result of this inward journey will be the inspiration for your drawing.

The special guided visualization for this project is based in part on the spiritual wisdom of the native American people. In the native American world view, the Earth is our mother, a living entity who gives life to all living things. Native Americans recognize the interdependence and interconnectedness of all natural phenomena—birds, animals, trees, fish, water, and air. All life is considered sacred and human beings are taught to respect and preserve the fabric of this interdependent life-support system. The following Navaho prayer expresses this wholesome desire to contemplate the Earth's beauty:

I came searching for you—
You and I will begin our return, my grandchild;

Encircling me sunwise with a rainbow,
He turns me, sunwise, toward himself,
And shows his compassion for me.

This is your home, my grandchild,
I have returned with you to your home,
Your home is yours again.
Your sacred mountains are yours again.
Your creatures are yours again.
The beauty of nature is yours again to enjoy, . . .

From the dwellings of the Holy Ones
Kind feelings will come to you as you go about in life.
Guided by these things, you shall find protection,
In all places as you live on, my grandchild, . . .
All is beautiful behind me
All is beautiful before me
All is beautiful below me
All is beautiful above me
All is beautiful all around me.
For I have been found and everything is beautiful.[2]

"POWER ANIMALS"—A VISIONARY QUEST

In native American tradition, as well as in other ancient cultures, spiritual leaders or shamans guide people on special inner journeys to meet what are called their "power animals." Spiritual rituals and the beating of drums induce altered states of consciousness, and in those states the seekers contact the spirit of the animals. They learn many things from their animal guides and gain information not normally accessible to their physical senses. Through this process the seekers make a sacred connection with the earth and establish a special relationship with the animals.

The spiritual tradition of the native Americans considers art a sacred practice. Inspired inner visions are manifested through art so that such knowledge can be brought into the physical plane. By using inspirational music and the special guided visualization in this chapter, you will make this kind of spiritual connection with the animals and the earth and manifest your own vision through drawing.

By doing the exercises and project you will:

- Learn how to blend and use colored pencils
- Be led on an inner journey to meet your own spiritual friends—a power fish, animal, and bird
- From this imagery develop a drawing on black paper that you will then color with your pencils

I will give you some basic instruction in color blending, but you will make all decisions relating to color. If you become fearful or indecisive, you need only ask your higher self or the power animals for help.

If you are like some of my students, you might doubt the validity of this approach! Let me anticipate such reactions and offer in response some comments from one of those same students after his first encounter with the guided visualization in this chapter:

When I was first told about the "journey" of the power animals, I thought it was really stupid and hoped none of my friends saw me. But during the middle of the journey, I felt free of everything . . . The part about flying in space was easy to believe, but when the power animals were supposed to talk [to me], that really confused me. I'm so used to being object oriented; I knew talking animals couldn't be real . . . But as I got into the project, I felt a little looser than when I started—nothing had to be proportional . . . imagination took over and I had the freedom to choose colors not of the real world.

If you feel an initial lack of trust in the inner journey process, just go through the motions until you feel yourself relax.

OVERCOMING FEAR OF THE IMAGINATION

Guided visualization encourages some of the most exciting work in drawing students that I have ever seen. As this chapter will prove to you, art and inspired vision come from within us. To accomplish these things, however, we must take the risk of dreaming and imagining. We must open our hearts, minds, and spirits to our innate creative potential.

The free use of imagination comes naturally to children. As we grow older, we often are taught to suppress our dreams and imaginations. If we study the lives of the great poets, artists, musicians, writers, and scientists, however, we find that dreaming and imagining have always played a vital part in stimulating their creative work. As a society we have suppressed this innate ability to dream and imagine, and in so doing we have inadvertently stunted our growth as human beings.

If one's imagination is suppressed early in life, reactivating the imaginative part of the self at a joyful and inspired level can be difficult. One woman in her fifties wrote movingly about her experience in grappling with this problem:

I tend to be precise, suffer a bit from being a perfectionist, and I hold back a lot. I often feel vulnerable. For that reason, the project [the power animal journey] was not easy for me. I am not in the habit of imagining, of creating. Daydreaming is the closest I ever came to fantasizing, especially about Prince Charming when I was younger. I didn't really get emotionally involved with the journey.

I had some nice ideas when listening to the music, and thinking my body could go straight to the stars, like a rocket. When coming down to Earth, I could see how beautiful it was, but I was not able to transfer any of these concepts or good feelings into my drawing. Often I was jealous of other students' work—I had a strong desire to be able to create the wonderful fantasy colors.

On a global level, when fears take over and the visionary powers are left underdeveloped, the creative energies of humankind are misdirected. All of life suffers. The native American spiritual philosophy, like the Hindu Tantric approach to art, holds that inner vision has the power to change the world. The art examples in this chapter demonstrate their creators' power to change their own perception of the world. This project will help you move past your fears so that you can enjoy the power and beauty of your vision.

SHARING THE INNER JOURNEY

To help you overcome any initial apprehension, enjoy the following stories by people who took the inner journey and shared their first-time experience of the visionary process:

I felt myself floating. My thoughts then flowed freely. As I got deeper into it, I felt a lot of control and power; images shot past me faster and more clearly. When I landed on the earth I could imagine hearing waves, birds, and other animal sounds.

The pictures that I imagined took several forms: photographs, moving pictures, cartoons, and even computer-enhanced animation. Maybe I was taking bits and pieces of what I saw in my life and was putting them together to create my own world. I felt excited during the journey. My mind's eyes were opened wide and wondering, trying to take in as much of the sights as I could.

—STANLEY (see figure C2-1)

Figure C2-1

Figure C2-2

Figure C2-3

Figure C2-4

Figure C2-5

Figure C2-6

Figure C2-7

Figure C2-8

Figure C2-9

Figure C2-11

Figure C2-10

Figure C2-12

Figure C2-13

Figure C2-17

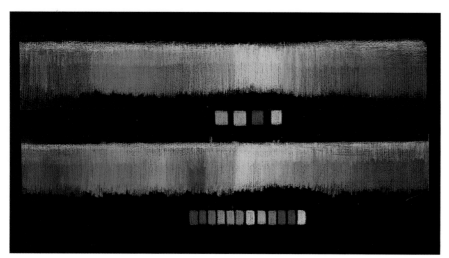

Figure C2-14. *Creating a rainbow with pencils. The top band of rainbow color was created by using only primary colors (aquamarine, canary yellow, and magenta) and a white pencil, as the four pencil color bars under the band indicate. The band beneath was created by blending and overlapping a full range of colored pencils in the order indicated by the colored bars underneath.*

Figure C2-15. *Exercises using complementary colors. The pencil color bars on the bottom left show the three complementary color combinations (yellow and violet, brice green and magenta, and orange and aquamarine) used to complete the color exercises in this illustration. The result from overlapping of these three combinations is illustrated on the right side. The box on the upper left shows spheres created by blending one of each complementary combination plus white.*

Figure C2-18. Complementary color wheel. Complementary colors are those colors opposite each other on the color wheel that produce neutral or brown tones when blended together.

Figure C2-16. Exercise using primary colors. The four pencil color bars on the bottom right indicate that the primary colors of aquamarine, canary yellow, and magenta, plus the white and black of the paper were the only colors used to complete this exercise. It demonstrates the versatility possible in using primary colors to achieve light and luminescent form. The point of this exercise is to create spheres by creatively blending all three colors in different proportions so that each sphere appears to be a different color with its own sense of light and volume.

Figure C2-19

Figure C2-20

Figure C2-21

Figure C2-22

When I started the project I was forced to use my own ideas with the animals and not rely on someone else's style [Nelson brought a visionary art book to class, which I asked him to put away]. At first I got angry because I felt I was being limited, yet now as I look back, I realize that I was set free. I began to express my own thoughts on paper and come up with my own style.

The journey itself was an exciting blast. I had never achieved an altered state like that before. I could actually see my animals, feel the sensation of flight, taste the fruit, and smell the salty air. It was an incredible sensory experience.

Being an incessant daydreamer, this project was easy for me to imagine. Yet I was stuck when it came to transferring my thoughts to paper. By using the power animals for help, I began to find it easier and easier to put what was in my mind on paper.

—NELSON (see figure C2-2)

During the visualization I imagined all the things in the world that I like and that I would like to see in one place on an island covered with palm trees, strawberries, and pyramids, surrounded by the sea. I could look out at the sky and see the earth spinning in orbit.

On this island I imagined three types of animals: a dolphin, Pegasus, and a cockatiel. These are my power animals. They all have their own personalities, and are overflowing with advice and wisdom. So when it came to coloring my picture, these animals told me—or rather allowed me—to see clearly what I had to do to make the picture come alive. They allowed me to see which colors I needed to use and where I needed to use them.

As I labored over my work, an excitement began to stir inside me, . . . because it was coming together so perfectly. The power animals weren't really telling me what to do, I was telling me what to do. I learned that I can trust my instincts about my art, and that is the most valuable thing of all.

—DAWN (see figure C2-8)

The journey for the search of our power animals surprised me. I never would have thought that I could pull some pictures out of a journey like that. Usually, the drawings I do are just from my head. Those drawings from my imagination come and go. Sometimes I get them, sometimes I don't. I think that if someone concentrates hard enough for the journey, that person could complete a picture every time. I liked this project particularly because of the colors I put into it. I think that colors are wonderful and fun when you start using them.

—Angelo (see figure C2-7)

I was very sceptical about tapping creativity through the imagination. I believed that everyone has some innate ability to draw or paint—some more, some less—and that this innate ability can be developed by practice and work. This practice and work, I thought, mainly involved concentration and logical analysis. In this visualization, the approach was to avoid logical analysis. I found it very difficult to imagine my power animal trip. My skeptical side kept saying, "This is silly." But when I could imagine, it was very real. I felt the water, saw colors, and the sunshine was hot on the island. The air was full of the fragrance of flowers, the sea, and dust. I could hear my footsteps and the sounds of insects and animals scurrying underfoot. I felt the wings of my power bird beat. And then I would open my eyes and say, "This is ridiculous."

As a result of this journey I find myself looking [at] the world differently. I enjoy looking more. Each scene has an interest, a dynamic I missed before. When I perceived analytically, I saw only the symbols and labels produced by my rational mind.

—Margaret (see figure C2-9)

At first I didn't think that this imaginative journey was practical, or that it would work. I even thought I would fall asleep in the process. But with the music and the visualization, even though I was in the room with thirty other people, I felt that I was actually floating in space and feeling the warm water. As I surfaced from the water I was actually out of breath. I felt the peacefulness of the deep water and I saw my power fish. Then, as I went to the land, I saw my power animal and bird. The hard part was trying to imagine my power animal as a fantasy, because it's pretty ridiculous for a deer to be orange. But while I was doing the project and had . . . to imagine the animals' colors again, the colors kept getting brighter and brighter. And after a while the colors didn't seem ridiculous anymore.

I had never used colored pencils before, but as I got further along with my work I started to have fun. Next time I work with colored pencils I won't be afraid.

—JENNIFER (see figure C2-4)

Most people take things for granted. Most people walk through life without thinking about what is surrounding them. Often we walk the dark side, and by this I mean that side of life that seems like an empty void in which we find ourselves running most of the time. This was my first drawing class and I have learned through this wonderful journey to see. And for me this is what it is all about— for all of us to learn to see, so that perhaps someday we will have a better understanding of the world around us, and about ourselves.

—PEDRO (see figure C2-5)

PART 1: LEARNING TO BLEND COLORED PENCILS

In chapter 2 you worked with colored paint pigments. In this chapter you will again explore the wonderful world of color, but this time you'll be mixing and blending colors directly on the paper, using pencils. To heighten the dramatic effects of colored pencils, you will work on black paper. In chapters 3 and 4, you worked on white paper with dark pencils and used the white as the light end of the scale. Here the black paper will serve as the darkest end of the scale, because it absorbs all light, until you add the color of the pencils to it.

Colored pencils are semitransparent. You will learn to produce color variations by blending layers of different colors. The semi-transparency of the pencils allows some of the other colors and the paper to show through.

Laying pure color onto black paper with some of the black showing through creates various shades of color. In chapter 2, you actually mixed a color with black or white paint to produce opaque scales. To create tints using pencils, your white pencil is blended on top and layered underneath colors. And you can make tones by using white-and-black pencils in conjunction with pure colors.

Just as in chapter 2, you will learn to blend primary, secondary, and tertiary colors to produce a rainbow spectrum. You will not, however, need to do a color wheel. Once more I have selected colors for you that are in harmony with both the visible light spectrum and the Ives color wheel. In this chapter your primary colors in pencils are called *magenta, canary yellow,* and *aquamarine,* because the pencil manufacturer labels its colors this way. Do not be confused by the labels, however. The word *aquamarine* refers to a turquoise color.

MATERIALS

- Scissors
- Pencil sharpener
- 3 sheets 18-by-24-inch newsprint paper
- 1 large sheet white transfer paper
- 1 large sheet translucent tracing paper
- #2 pencil
- Pink Pearl Eraser
- Ruler
- Small roll of masking tape
- Records or tapes of inspirational music

American paper

- 2 sheets 19-by-25-inch black Strathmore Charcoal paper, black Canson Ingres Vidalon, Canson Mitentes black charcoal drawing paper, or a large sheet of Arches black cover stock

European paper

- 2 sheets 700 mm x 500 mm black Daler Ingres Rowney charcoal paper (made in England), or black Canson Ingres Vidalon 50 x 65 cm, or Canson Mitentes drawing paper (made in Annonay, France). There are other black pastel papers in Europe. You may need to experiment with them to see which side of the paper is best to draw on for creating the most radiant scale of light.

- Berol Prismacolor or Berol Karisma Colour Pencils (made in England).

  The following represent the basic primary colors plus white:

  #938 white drawing pencils (three of these)

  #905 aquamarine   #930 magenta
  #916 canary yellow

  Add the following for the exercises calling for a richer palatte:

  #903 true blue   #910 true green
  #913 green brice or spring green   #918 orange
  #923 scarlet lake   #932 violet
  #933 blue-violet   #935 black

The following are optional Berol pencil colors. You may wish to use these pencils in your final drawing. These are soft pastel-like colors, similar to some of the soft colors you created by adding white paint to colored paint in chapter 2:

  #904 light blue   #934 lavender
  #956 light violet   #929 pink
  #939 flesh   #928 blush
  #992 light aqua

EXERCISE 1: PROCEDURES FOR BLENDING PRIMARY COLORS USING PENCILS

Blending colored pencils is not much different from using other drawing pencils. In this first exercise you will practice making smoothly blended transitions from one colored pencil to another. When you do the following exercise, be conscious of the pressure you use on the pencil. Heavy pressure leaves more pigment color on the paper and allows less of the black to show through. Lighter pressure leaves less color and lets more of the black paper show through. Experiment until you find a pressure that suits your artistic temperament and expression.

Berol Prisma color pencils are constructed with a waxy base. I have found that if you apply heavy pressure to the color too soon, it is difficult to layer other colors on top because the surface becomes too glossy to work on due to its waxy texture. If you find it difficult to layer color on top of other color, try lightly sanding the surface of the color with fine mesh steel wool to take away some of the gloss. These colored pencils do not erase. To make changes you must add other colors over what you have already put down.

1. Take out a sheet of black paper and the following colored pencils: white, aquamarine, canary yellow, and magenta. In this first exercise you will blend the three primary colored pencils in logical order to create a rainbow of color on black paper.

2. Fold your sheet of black paper in half. Using the scissors, cut the paper in half along the fold line. Put aside one-half of the paper. Place your paper horizontally in front of you. Use your white pencil to draw a quarter- to a half-inch-wide band of white across the full width of your paper near the top edge. You'll use this strip of white first to see what your primary colors look like when placed over white pencil on black paper.

3. Pick up your yellow pencil. Starting in the middle of the page, draw a yellow vertical band, approximately two inches long and two inches wide, so that the yellow goes over the white pencil and onto the black paper. The intensity of your yellow will depend on the pressure you use on the pencil. If you use light pressure, your yellow will be pale and the black paper will show through the color. Heavier pressure on the pencil will create a more brilliant color.

4. Pick up your magenta pencil and draw a vertical two-inch-wide band to the right of the yellow. Then blend the magenta onto a third of the yellow band. You will get an orange color. To create a smooth blend going from yellow to yellow-orange, orange, red, and back to magenta, you can blend the two colors of yellow and magenta in several different ways. You can add yellow on top of the magenta that you put over the yellow to make a lighter orange. To produce a red, you may need to add more magenta to a section of your orange area. Experiment with the different ways to put these two colors over and under each other. By starting with a medium pressure on your pencils, you can build layers of transparent color upon color. Remember, if your pressure is too heavy when you start, you will produce a glossy coating of pencil, and later you will find that it will be difficult to add other colors to the top of a glossy surface. Before proceeding to the next part, make sure you have created a smooth transitional scale going from yellow to magenta. Study figure C2-14.

5. When you are finished, take your aquamarine pencil and draw a two-inch-wide vertical band of aquamarine to the left of the yellow band.

6. Blend the aquamarine over part of the yellow to get various yellow-greens and greens working back to the blue. Leave a small band of pure yellow between the oranges and greens.

7. Next, draw a two-inch-wide band of magenta to the left of the blue. Create a blue-violet on this end by taking your aquamarine pencil and blending it on top of the magenta you just put down. With the blue on top of the magenta, more blue shows, thus creating an optical mix of blue-violet color.

8. Next, draw a two-inch-wide band of aquamarine blue next to the magenta on the right-hand side of the paper. To create red-violet and complete the rainbow, color a layer of magenta over the aquamarine. The magenta being placed on top of the blue creates a red-violet.

9. Now take out your white Prisma pencil. Proceeding lengthwise at the bottom half of your rainbow strip, use your white pencil to draw a narrow strip of white on top of your rainbow colors. Notice how the colors can be lightened by putting white on top. Notice the difference between putting white *under* the color and *on top* of the color. Each effect is different, allowing you greater latitude in color expression with pencils.

EXERCISE 2: BLENDING A FULL ASSORTMENT OF PENCILS

1. When you have completed exercise 1, make another rainbow spectrum by adding the following pencils to your primary colors to create a richer palette:

932 violet   # 933 blue-violet
903 true blue   # 905 aquamarine
910 true green   # 913 green brice or spring green
916 canary yellow   # 918 orange
923 scarlet lake   # 930 magenta
938 white.

Line up these pencils side-by-side in front of you in the order given.

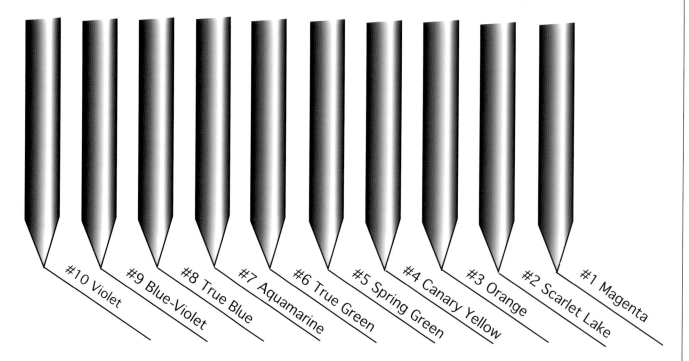

Figure 5-1. Line drawing for pencil order exercise 2. For further clarification, study the pencil color code arrangement in figure C2-14 of the color insert.

2. On the same sheet of paper and below the rainbow strip that you just completed, draw another narrow strip of white across the width of the paper. You will do the exercise this time using the full range of colored pencils, but first, arrange them in the right sequence (see figure 5-1). Start with yellow in the middle as you did in the first exercise.

3. With yellow as your center color, take your orange pencil and draw a band to the left of yellow. Blend some orange onto part of the yellow to produce yellow-orange. When you finish, take your scarlet red and draw a band next to the orange and blend some of the scarlet red on top of the orange. Finally, to complete this end of the scale, take your magenta and draw a band next to your scarlet lake and then blend some of your magenta onto part of the scarlet lake.

4. Now you will complete the rest of the rainbow. Take your green brice pencil and draw a band to the right of the canary yellow. Blend some of the green brice onto the canary yellow. With your true green pencil, draw a band next to the green brice and blend some of the true green onto part of the green brice. Next, take your aquamarine and draw a band next to the true green, blending some of the aquamarine onto part of the true green. Take your true blue pencil, draw a band next to the aquamarine, and blend it onto part of the aquamarine. Continue this blending process using bands of blue-violet next to the true blue and violet next to the blue-violet. To make a red-violet, put aquamarine next to the violet and blend magenta onto the aquamarine. When you have finished, check to see that you have created smooth transitions that blend to a full rainbow scale. Then draw a narrow band of white across the bottom half of your rainbow strip to see how the colors change when white is laid on top of them.

Note: Advanced exercises using colored pencils on black paper to create light-filled art can be found in my book, *MANDALA: Luminous Symbols for Healing*, pages 84-90.

EXERCISE 3: BLENDING COMPLEMENTARY COLORS

This exercise will help you experiment further with colors. You will learn to mix the three primary colors with their complementary colors. Quite simply, complementary colors are those colors opposite each other on the color wheel. Look at figure C2-18 (color insert) and you will note that the opposite of magenta is green, the opposite of turquoise is orange, and the opposite of yellow is violet. Nature displays many complementary color combinations, especially in flowers. Red and purple flowers with green foliage and yellow pansies with violet centers are but two of many examples.

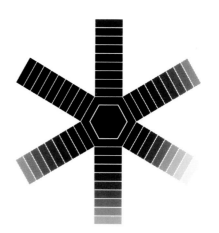

As you can see in figure C2-18, when complementary colors are mixed together, they produce neutral or gray tones. These gray tones are different from those you made by mixing black-and-white paint together. Each complementary combination of gray or neutral tones will be influenced by the colors you mixed together. For instance, magenta and green neutral grays will look different from turquoise and orange mixes.

These complementary mixes will afford you an even greater latitude for making dynamic color combinations. The exercise below will teach you how to mix three specific sets of complementary colors, but you'll be able to treat any colors that are opposite each other on the color wheel in a similar manner. After you complete this exercise, feel free to experiment with other complementaries, referring to the color wheel (figure C1-16) as a guide.

1. Take out the other half sheet of black paper that you set aside, your ruler, and the following pencils: magenta, green brice, violet, canary yellow, aquamarine, orange, and white. With your white pencil and ruler, draw three two-inch squares on your black paper. Arrange the squares so that they are near each other because you will be doing several exercises on this same paper.

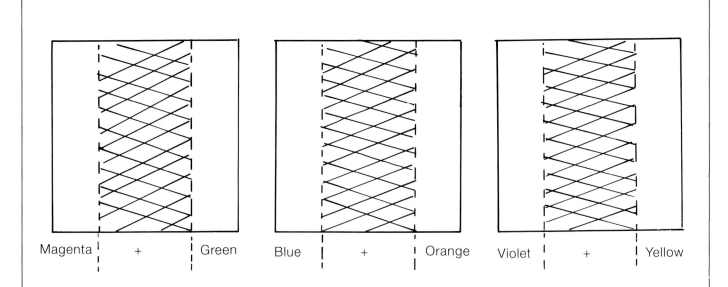

Magenta + Green   Blue + Orange   Violet + Yellow

2. Using your white pencil, draw a narrow band of white along the top edge of each square. Next, take out your magenta and true-green pencils. In one square draw a band of magenta that fills half the square and covers half the white strip. Next, fill the other half of the square with green and cover the other half of the white strip. You now have the two complementaries next to each other. To produce neutral tones you will need to overlap them, but leave a small strip of each pure color on either end. Using light pressure on your green pencil, blend green onto half the magenta strip. Then, using light pressure on your magenta pencil, blend magenta onto half the band of green. Be aware that the pressure of your pencils will determine the quality of your neutral colors. Go over these colors until you get a neutral or gray quality to the two color mixes. Then use your white pencil to put a narrow band of white across the bottom of your square, showing that still more combinations are possible when you add white to your complementary mixes.

3. Go to the next square. This time, blend your aquamarine and orange pencils following the same procedures as above. When you finish, follow the same process in the third square, using your yellow and violet pencils.

Figure 5-2. Line drawing for complementary mixes. This line drawing illustrates the combinations of overlapping complementary colors. For further clarification, study figure C2-15 of the second color insert.

EXERCISE 4: CREATING FORM AND LIGHT USING COLORS

1. Next, on the same paper, use your ruler and white pencil to draw two 4-by-4-inch squares near each other. In each square draw three or more circles freehand using your white pencil. This exercise is very much like the circle exercise in chapter 3. There you dissolved the lines and created a form that had light and luminescence. The idea here is exactly the same, except that now you are using colored pencils. In the first square you will use only the three primary colors plus black and white. In the second square you will use the three primary colors plus their complements and additions of black and white.

2. Take out your black, white, and primary colors of magenta, canary yellow, and aquamarine. In the first square you will do an exercise using these three primary colors plus your white-and-black pencil. Each circle in the first box will use all three colors but in different proportions. This exercise will help you see the results of intermixing and overlapping of primary colors with black and white. Before you begin, try sitting quietly, closing your eyes, and visualizing the colored pencils as being different colors of light and energy. *Visualize the colored pencils as a series of colored rainbow lights.*

3. Before you start coloring your circles, close your eyes and imagine objects that are round and full of colored light. Do not begin until you can imagine them. One ball will contain mostly yellow with small additions of the other two colors plus white. The next ball will consist primarily of aquamarine with small additions of the magenta and yellow. The third ball will consist primarily of magenta with small additions of the yellow and aquamarine.

4. Use black-and-white pencil over or under the colors to create a full range of value changes, going from light to dark. As you work, think about where you want the light source to be. To create light or bright areas, use white with the colors. To create dark values, use black with your colors. Experiment using only these colors to create an interesting background for your colored spheres. (Study figure C2-16, illustration of circles using primary colors.) Now you are ready to begin.

5. Go to the next square after you have completed the primary color exercise. In each of the three circles in this second square, blend one of each of the complementary color mixes, plus white and black. In one circle blend magenta and green, in the second blend violet and yellow, and in the third blend aquamarine and orange. Again, add black-and-white pencil to create a full range of values in your spheres and to create a sense of light and three-dimensional form. After you have blended the complementary mixes, feel free to experiment with other color blends. (Study figure C2-15, illustration of circles using complementary colors.)

PART 2: AN INNER JOURNEY TO MEET YOUR SPIRITUAL FRIENDS

Now you have learned the basic skills necessary to draw on paper the images from your inner journey. Ideally, the following inner-journey visualization should be played on a tape player, but if you do not have the tape, ask a friend to read it to you slowly while playing soft, meditative music. It is important for the person who reads this visualization to go slowly and to pause briefly at the ellipses (. . .) in order to give your imagination time to see images.

Find a quiet place to sit where you will not be distracted. While you are on this journey, let your imagination flow freely. Do not worry if the animals, birds, or fish you see are different in color or form from those you see in the outer world. These are your power animals. If you find that your power animals talk to you, be open to the experience. In the realm of imagination anything is possible. The images you see on this journey will be used as a resource for the picture you will draw later.

• Before you begin your visualization, have a piece of newsprint paper and pencil nearby. After you finish the visualization, quickly sketch the images of your birds, animals, fish, and any other images that came to you and write in as much detail as possible about the experiences and the feelings you had on this journey. If you forget what you imagined, sit quietly and take yourself back on the journey to review what you saw. This step is the first in creating your finished drawing. Your notes and drawing can be quite crude and raw at this point. Later you will have time to refine your drawings.

• After you have finished recording the journey and images, proceed with the project as outlined.

Vision of A Peaceful Planet
A VISUALIZATION

With your eyes closed, sit comfortably in a chair with your hands resting in your lap and your feet flat on the floor. Imagine a ball or a prism of rainbow light at the top of your head. Now bring that energy down through your head into your brain, down your spine into your lungs, and into your heart. You will need to open up the heart to go on this journey, so it's important for you to watch as that prism of energy expands. Open your heart, feel a lot of love, and realize that you are wonderful and great. Let the light and love enter your heart; visualize it filling the whole room in which you are sitting. See how far into space you can push that energy. Now bring that energy down through your stomach and into your other organs, down through your legs, and into the ground. Feel the stream of warm energy from the top of your head flowing all the way through your body and into the ground. Now guide that energy back up through your feet, up the back of your legs, and bring it slowly back up through your spine. Finally bring it up into your head. Imagine a rainbow of energy filling your whole being.

You are now ready to go on the journey. Feel yourself lifting slowly and softly off the ground . . . Imagine that you are now floating freely in outer space . . . Feel peace, love, and oneness with all the cosmos. Look around you. Become aware of the glowing beauty of the galaxy . . . What do you see in this galaxy? Try to remember that you are made out of the atoms of this light . . . Imagine yourself drifting slowly toward the Earth. See the Earth the way the astronauts saw it as they viewed it from the moon: as a splendid blue pearl, spinning gently in a universe of energy. . . Come closer now to the Earth and begin to see the vast expanse of ocean . . . See yourself floating over this magnificent blue-green ocean . . . Ahead of you is a beautiful tropical island . . . Approach this island . . . As you look down on the water and the island, find a place in the ocean where you would like to descend . . . Slowly go into the water and feel it close gently around you . . . look around you . . . notice the world of undersea life that surrounds you.

As you are swimming, notice the fish swimming in front of you. One in particular seems special to you . . . It comes close to you. This is your power fish. Notice its color and any distinguishing characteristics . . . In your mind's eye, open your heart with love and send a beam of love to your special friend . . . Sense the warmth and friendship of your newfound friend . . . You both now swim off together. Your power fish is leading you toward the island . . . You see an underwater cave and you both swim into the cave. Your fish guides you to the end of the cave and you see a light coming into the water from above you . . . You realize that your fish has brought you to the island so you can meet your power animal. You bid good-bye to your fish and swim toward the light . . . toward the surface of the island.

As you step onto the land, notice the surrounding area. What is the vegetation like? . . . Notice the flowers and trees . . . What kind of day is it? . . . Is it warm and sunny? Can you smell the tropic growth? . . . In front of you there is a path. This path will lead you to your power animal. As you are going along the path, stop and gather presents for your power animal if you wish . . . Now you notice your special animal ahead on the path . . . What does your power animal look like? . . . What color or colors do you imagine your animal to have? . . . With warmth and love in your heart, present your gifts to your power animal . . . At this time your animal may want to talk with you. Listen for any words that your animal has to share with you . . .

You and your new friend continue on the path together. Your power animal leads you to the top of a hill . . . You realize that you are being led to meet your power bird. When you reach the top of the hill, notice the view that opens up to you . . . What do you see from this height? . . . It is now time to say good-bye to your power animal. You give thanks to your animal for all the knowledge you have received. As you stand on the hill, you watch your power animal descend to the path below.

You are not alone for long on the top of this hill . . . Suddenly your power bird comes into view . . . What color or colors do you see? What size and shape is your bird? Slowly you draw nearer to your power bird and, keeping you heart open, you look for a gift to present to your power bird . . . Present your gift to your power bird and listen for any message your bird has for you—words of wisdom meant just for you . . . You and your power bird view the horizon together. You feel a great sense of peace and love . . . Now it is time to leave this island, so you thank your power bird for being your friend . . . Lift yourself once more into the universe and feel the abundance of love and peace and remember all that you imagined and heard. You will bring back with you these images for inspiration. Your journey is at an end. In your mind's eye, see yourself sitting in the chair in the room you left before your journey. You are back now, sitting in your chair in your room. Slowly and gently, when you are ready, open your eyes, and in the silence quickly write and draw all you saw, heard, and felt.

PROJECT: DRAWING FROM YOUR INNER VISION

In this part of the creative process you will learn how to express in dynamic drawing the images that came to you as a result of this imaginary journey. To make an arresting picture from your experience you will develop an asymmetrical or symmetrical composition and learn to overlap and collage the images you saw. In the first part of this process you will draw and cut out silhouettes of your power bird, fish, and animal. To create an interesting picture plane, you will apply the elements of good design you learned in chapter 1. In previous chapters you applied elements of good design to abstract, nonfigurative images. In this project you will apply this knowledge to recognizable imagery.

MATERIALS

Use materials listed in part 1 of this project.

PROCEDURES

1. Take out out the images you sketched from your journey, a sheet of newsprint paper, a ruler, an eraser, tracing paper, scissors, and a pencil. Cut out silhouettes (outlines only) of various sizes of your animal, bird, and fish. If your power animals are unlike anything you have seen in nature, draw the silhouettes of these animals, using your imagination only. Refer to the sketches you drew after your journey if you need to. Your views of the animals can be from the front, back, side, or a combination of all three.

2. If what you saw in your imagination reminded you of animals, birds, or fish from nature, feel free to use pictures from books or magazines for reference. Place your tracing paper on top of the image and with your pencil trace the outline only. Do not copy any details from the reference materials. Look for a variety of shapes and sizes. If you have access to a photocopy machine that can enlarge and reduce images, try enlarging and reducing your images to get silhouettes of various shapes and sizes. Then cut out the various shapes with your scissors.

3. Next, take a piece of newsprint paper, and using your ruler and pencil, draw a 16-by-20-inch rectangle. This paper will be your draft paper for creating your line drawing. Later you will trace this line drawing onto your black paper. (The 16-by-20-inch rectangle is a suggested format size only. You may make it larger, but not larger than your black paper.)

4. Arrange your silhouettes inside the format of your newsprint paper in a way that you find interesting. You may find that some of your images are too big for the format. If so, draw them to a smaller scale. Use two or more silhouettes and various sizes of your bird, fish, and animal.

5. Begin your drawing by overlapping silhouette forms and tracing around these shapes with a pencil. After you have traced a number of shapes, erase some of the overlap lines to give a sense of depth and perspective to your picture. The process is like putting a puzzle of many shapes together. Continue to arrange and rearrange these silhouetted shapes and, with your pencil, draw interconnecting lines of landscape horizons, trees, and vegetation, until an interesting story composite begins to emerge. The aim is to establish the skeletal structure of your drawing composition. In chapters 1, 2, and 3, you developed abstract line compositions before you used paint or pencils. You are doing the same thing here, but you are using recognizable imagery. If the skeletal framework exhibits exciting line patterns and shapes, the process of completing a dynamic composition becomes much easier, since the direction is already established. Study the student examples of line compositions in figures 5-3 and 5-4.

6. Do not isolate a silhouette in the middle of the page without regard to the overall composition. Your outline shapes should be connected to and integrated with the rest of the picture. Avoid putting details in your line drawing. Later, after you have transferred your line drawing to black paper and have begun to color it, you can add details.

Figure 5-3. In this student's line composition, some of the lines were erased to create a sense of depth where the shapes overlapped. Repetition and size variation of silhouetted shapes were used to create an interesting composition on the black paper. See the final drawing in figure C2-10 of the second color insert.

Figure 5-4. This is another example of a student's silhouette composition traced in white pencil on black paper. The composition is composed of images from the power animal journey. Note that no details were added at this point in the process. See the final drawing in figure C2-8 of the second color insert.

7. When you feel you have finished, stand back and look at your composition. Ask yourself the following questions: Is the composition visually interesting? Does it begin to tell a story? Do you need to add other lines or shapes to create more movement or complexity? If your composition is boring to you, how can you rearrange your design and line drawing to make it more interesting? Review the Basic Elements of Good Design in chapter 1.

8. When you are satisfied with your composition, transfer this drawing to the black paper. Take out your white transfer paper, the large sheet of black paper, a pencil, and a ruler. Lay your black paper down in front of you and position the white transfer paper on top of the black paper with the waxy side down. Place your newsprint drawing on top of the transfer paper with the drawing face up. Place several pieces of masking tape on each end of the papers to secure them so that they do not move while you trace your drawing onto black paper.

9. Using medium pressure on your pencil, trace over the lines you have drawn on the newsprint paper. After you finish tracing your line drawing, carefully lift up part of your newsprint and white transfer paper to see if you missed any areas and to make sure that your image has transferred to the black paper. If you did the procedures correctly, you should see an exact copy of your drawing on black paper; only the lines and shapes will be in white. Make sure you have also traced your rectangular 16-by-20-inch format lines onto the black paper. These lines determine the edges of your picture frame. When you have finished tracing, remove the newsprint and transfer paper from the black paper.

10. You are now ready to color your final drawing. Take out all of your colored pencils and all of the color exercises you did on black paper. Before you begin, review these concepts:

   • When you are coloring, avoid using any single color alone. Always overlap and mix colors as you did for the exercises. For example, if you were going to use red in an area, overlap other colors, such as yellows and oranges or blues and greens, onto the red. Remember, too, that you can reverse this process by starting out with either the yellows and oranges or blues and greens and finish by layering a predominant red on top of the other colors.

▪ Continue to think of your colors as radiant light—your vision is light, color, and truth.

▪ The objective is to dissolve the lines of your drawing and to create a picture that is full of luminescent forms.

▪ As you work, you may find that the vision changes from what you actually saw. Welcome these changes as part of the creative process. Allow yourself the freedom to change the concept as you go along.

▪ As you are coloring, you can add other details to your drawing. Be open to following your heart, imagination, and intuition.

11. Before you actually begin coloring, it is very important to repeat the guided visualization for your inner journey. It will reinforce your vision and stimulate your memory for details, colors, and the original feelings you had. If, during the process of realizing your final drawing on black paper, you feel unsure or tense about what colors to use or what direction to take, go back inside yourself and ask your power animals to help you. Think of these power animals as part of your higher self. Keep your heart open and loving. Realize that power and knowledge is within you, and that your vision is perfect and adds to the beauty and truth of the world.

12. Hang up your drawing periodically while you are working on it. Remember that gaining distance from your drawing will help you to see what you are doing and to identify areas that need further work. Don't be timid about your use of color and don't be afraid to experiment with color. If areas seem weak and flat in tone, apply more color and pressure to your pencils. Since Prisma color pencils do not erase, all changes will be made by adding other colors. Do not give up because you put down a color different than the one you intended. Use your intuition to lead you to other colors to lay on top of it to make it more interesting. Above all, make coloring your composition a joyous experience. When you are finished, hang up your completed work in a place where you can see it every day.

WHAT HAVE YOU LEARNED?

This project focused your consciousness inward, where you found the spirit of the earth and celebrated its abundance. Use the inner vision you manifested in your drawing to remind yourself always of that sacred relationship. With this project completed, you should have a new appreciation for the Navaho prayer quoted earlier:

All is beautiful behind me
All is beautiful before me
All is beautiful below me
All is beautiful above me
All is beautiful all around me.
For I have been found and everything is beautiful.

SUGGESTED READING

Devall, Bill, and George Sessions. *Deep Ecology: Living as If Nature Mattered.* Salt Lake City: Gibbs M. Smith, 1985.
Harner, Michael. *The Way of the Shaman: A Guide to Power and Healing.* New York: Harper & Row, 1980.

NOTES

1. John G. Neihardt, *When the Tree Flowered* (New York: Macmillan, 1951), 53.
2. Ralph Metzner, *Opening to Inner Light* (Los Angeles: J. P. Tarcher, 1986), 138–139.

## CHAPTER 6

Journey to the Hall of Wisdom

*When Man integrates Himself and Works as a Whole, authority vanishes;
henceforth every Man may converse with God and be a King and Priest in his
own house.*

—William Blake[1]

A man's wisdom makes his face to shine.

—Ecclesiastes

BECOMING A CHANNEL FOR SPIRITUAL TRUTH

FOR WILLIAM BLAKE, the true artist worked holistically—that is, integrating the mind, body, and spirit. Blake believed that this fully integrated person could become a creative channel for spiritual truths. Such an artist would be able to express his or her own part of a larger spiritual reality. Supporting Blake's view, the biographies of great philosophers, spiritual leaders, artists, musicians, writers, and scientists show that they sometimes experienced themselves as channels under the direct guidance of God or a special spiritual guide or muse.

After I had used an integrated approach to teaching art for several years, I began to wonder if ordinary students could access these deeper spiritual levels. To answer my question, I decided to experiment with the visualization and imaginative drawing project that you are about to do. I gave this project to a beginning drawing class as their final assignment for the remaining three class periods. The students did not have to master any new drawing skills. They would need only to apply the knowledge and skills they had already learned.

I created a guided visualization that was an imaginary journey to a more highly evolved planet than ours. Students visualized loving and peaceful people there and a spiritual guide on the planet who took them to the Hall of Wisdom. My objective for visiting the Hall of Wisdom was to explore more deeply the ancient philosophies that maintain that all knowledge and wisdom reside within us. By having students visualize a planet of peaceful loving people, they could transcend their fears and begin imagining the actual ways to create peace, love, and harmony on this planet.

I was amazed at the beauty, profoundity, and clarity of the students' visions. Their insights covered a range of subjects: art, philosophy, and invention, as well as the need for unselfish love and peaceful use of the earth's resources. Equally moving was the look on their faces after the journey—radiant with love, light, and understanding. Wisdom and truth have often come from the least likely sources. Now I witnessed it coming from ordinary, loving, unpretentious people from many cultures taking a beginning class in drawing.

TAPPING THE WISDOM WITHIN

This chapter illustrates some of their unusual stories and drawings. More important are the implications of their insights for humanity. These students allowed me to include their stories and pictures as a gift to you—a gift of love, vision, and truth brought forth from their deepest selves.

In his Hall of Wisdom, Angelo was shown a gallery of art containing many of the great art works done on the earth (see figure 6-1). His spiritual guide told him that the paintings on earth were imitations and that the real paintings and the inspiration for them came from this more evolved planet. This concept of images inspired by spiritual beings or expanded states of consciousness is not new. Numerous artists throughout history and in all cultures—the yogi, the shaman, and many individual artists like

Figure 6-1

William Blake, Hildegard von Bingen, and the contemporary "visionary" artists—have experienced the feeling that they are channels for divine vision.

Another student, Christine, learned from her guide that meditation was an important practice to quiet the mind in order to solve problems and develop creativity. She shares her experiences:

In my vision there was a city with white houses that all looked alike, except for the brightly colored flowers in the windows. The road led to a huge golden dome. My guide, Hom, showed me many beautiful musical instruments in the golden Hall of Wisdom. The people sitting inside looked as if they were meditating. Hom explained that these people practiced sitting quietly to develop their imagination and creativity in order to solve problems and get ideas. Instead of watching TV as we do, these people spent time thinking and seemed very energetic and peaceful at the same time. There were children, many people in the streets, and many smiling faces.

—CHRISTINE

Emma had a profound spiritual experience as a result of her journey to the Hall of Wisdom. The wisdom she received taught her that she could be anything she wanted to be. Her fears about becoming an artist dissolved when she grasped the truth that to be an artist was to be alive and the artist's purpose was to function consciously as a divine cocreator in the universe.

In this journey I was given knowledge. I was shown that I can be what I wish to be. What I saw was harmony and wisdom. I saw balance and aesthetics. I saw the beauty in the simple flower. The clean balance of a stone pillar. The wisdom of the ages. To become a part of that, to develop my skills, to be at peace and know that I have given my soul. That is what my goal is.

I asked my guide if I was making the correct choice in pursuing a career in art. My uncertainty was overwhelming at the onset of the journey, but I found my answer and have regained my confidence. The act of getting in touch with one's self through inner journey is a beneficial experience. What I saw in the golden building was . . . peace and harmony, love and beauty; art eternal and alive.

—EMMA

On her journey, Pantha met a female guide whom she felt she had known in past lifetimes (see figure C2-13). This guide showed her that the medium for painting was light. Even though Pantha's drawing was done in pencils, it looks like light and luminescent paint. Her drawing captures the essence of her journey—the power to create or paint one's reality from light and energy.

In my vision, my eye is tuned to color. All the things I see have an inner light. When we took the journey to the other world, I went back to a place I've been before. My guide was female, dark, and beautiful. Over the years that I've known her, she has changed colors and even gender. But she remains the same. Her animal [power animal], like mine, is the panther. The jars in my drawing are also very old. In my guide's little shop, there is no color. It's all dark, save for the jars of light, myself, and her. The jars are many things to me. They are light, the ability to fly, sensuality . . . they are all the things I want to be and the things I am. When things are hard I only have to let the light enter and things grow warm . . . I hear words of wisdom; sensuality and strength are beauty. My art strives for both.

—PANTHA

Stanley, at age nineteen, demonstrated unusual talent as an emerging visionary artist (see figure C2-17). He was able to review the images from his inner journey at will for several days after the visualization. He did this to help himself recall details to use in his drawing. His vision gives insight into what the practice of art might hold for the artist. On his highly evolved planet, the artists had developed great mental power to create and interact with their art.

Inside the hall, the first thing my guide showed me was a very plain-looking pencil inside a glass display case. For these people the pencil has been the basic tool of the artist for thousands of years. The guide explained that the pencil is a primitive and simple tool, yet it can render art just as beautifully as commercial graphic computers can. The people of this planet felt compelled to put it in a place where people could honor and admire it. They didn't put it in the museum because they thought it was a relic that no longer had a place in the art world, but they wanted to show their appreciation for its existence.

Other cases contained different objects such as an ink dip pen, paint brushes, a palette, and also a contraption that looked like an airbrush, but I did not get a good look at any of them. She [my guide] knew I would be drawn to the pencil. It was the tool I've been drawing with the longest. The huge gold sculpture in the background was hard to make out, but my guide let me know that it was very old and the artist said it signified the galaxy's passion for art, so she dedicated it to all artists.

The first grotesque figure on the left popped into my head when I asked my guide about my fears. I think that figure represents fear. Fear is in the Hall of Art because all artists have experienced the fear of screwing up a drawing or work of art. Fear was ugly, but not ugly enough to scare me. I guess that means it doesn't have a firm grip on me.

The last thing [my guide] showed me was also the most impressive. It was a giant 20-by-20-foot video screen floating in midair. It is the latest toy for artists. Somehow the screen is hooked up to a computer that can scan brain waves. The images in the user's mind can be projected onto the screen. He can freeze the image there and do anything to it that he wants: change the colors, erase parts, or even enlarge the image. It's literally drawing with the mind as compared to drawing with the mouse, which is our latest computer toy.

They scanned my brain without telling me and bits and pieces of my most recent visual stimuli flashed on the screen, things like the futuristic skyscraper, my spaceship, and my guide's face, but most of the time there was snow on the screen. I couldn't see any images at all. I guess I didn't know how to use it. The image on the screen in my picture is rainbow light, the energy in all of us.

—STANLEY

Liem came here from Vietnam. Liem received a gift of invention from his guide. He had told me of his dream to be a car designer. He asked me if I could suggest a place where he could study car designing. I did not have an answer, but as a result of his journey, Liem went a step beyond a traditional school for car designing. He learned from his inner guide how to design an

advanced car (see figure C2-19). Liem's experience of receiving specific information through spiritual guidance parallels the stories of famous inventors and composers. The following is Liem's description of his journey:

I was floating in space, seeing the planets covered by beautiful colors and radiating energy. Seated in a spaceship, I flew at great speed toward a planet that was sending out extraordinary energy.

Right after I landed on that strange planet, I saw a group of aliens greeting me. They were all in silver uniforms so bright that it blurs my eyes. Many wonderful colored rays of energy radiated from them. They were all shorter than humans, and their heads were very large compared to their bodies. One of them came toward me. He was much taller than the rest. With a friendly smile, he introduced himself as Forbinh and shook my hand. Right at that moment I felt his energy go into my body and felt my eyes become brighter.

Forbinh showed me around the city in a very high-tech car. He drove so fast that it scared me, but I started to realize that it was safe. All the other cars around us also traveled very fast, yet they all were very controlled. I noticed that all the cars could make a sharp turn without reducing their speed. Forbinh stopped the car in front of a golden palace, and we went into the palace. There was nothing inside except a car—a space car—a beautiful high-tech automobile. He explained to me all the details of the vehicle and suggested that I remember everything about the car and design a similar one when I get back to earth.

—LIEM

Yet Wah came to this country from mainland China. In his mid-thirties, he had only ten years of formal education. Yet Wah's heart, spirit, and vision speak wisely about the need for unselfish sharing of the earth's resources and the need for us to open our hearts to love so we can achieve peace on the earth. In his vision he saw that the planets were abundantly rich in minerals and that the universe was vast and borderless.

I saw some spaceships, satellites, and rockets. The planets were rotating in the space. This was a borderless, quiet, and peaceful universe. My guide showed me that there were lots of minerals among the planets. At this moment, I thought about our world where lots of people . . . were so busy working for their wealth, and some people lost their lives because of money. Also, people were fighting each other on earth because of different opinions. Some countries had wars because of a small piece of land that belonged to them. It is so foolish! Why don't we share our love with all the people instead of violence? Why don't we use our energy to research the advanced technologies and scientific expertise essential for humans?

—Yet Wah

Geng-Lan was born in China and had been in this country a little more than two years when she started taking my beginning drawing class. Geng-Lan came back from her inner journey with her face radiating love and light. In her vision she saw that the people on the planet had no energy problems, as they used solar energy. Geng-Lan shares her vision:

I was brought into a new and strange world. I was like a butterfly, flying out of the earth. Pretty soon I reached another planet. The person who welcomed me was a little tiny lady. She told me that she was a bird, but in human form. I followed her into a rainbow building. In the building, she pointed out a heavy machine and let me look through a little hole. Looking through the hole I realized that the buildings on that planet were all tanks designed to adjust to variable temperatures. These buildings were warm and saving space.

When I looked carefully, I noticed that there was a parabola-shaped machine on the top of each tank. My guide said that they didn't use any kind of energy except solar energy; therefore, they didn't need to worry about energy problems. On the second floor of the building she showed me a nuclear test. She said that the test was not used in wars but for changing temperature and fields. She also introduced me to the form of the planet. The planet was purple outside, yellow in the middle, and had a red center.

—Geng-Lan

Unlike the other students, Jennifer saw no buildings in her vision (see figure C2-20). She had a powerful spiritual experience that gave her insights into the philosophy of reincarnation and other teachings of ancient wisdom:

It was a beautiful planet with a bluish green moon. The land was mysterious-looking, with rocky mountains and steep cliffs. I didn't see any cities because it was a primitive planet. The people didn't live in buildings like ours. They seemed to just exist. But even though they lived a primitive life, I found out that they were far more advanced than we were in wisdom and knowledge of life.

I met my friend Antera, who was beautiful. I will say "he" but actually he is neither man nor woman. He was energy itself. He was glowing like gold and looked so peaceful. When I saw him I thought he'd burn me, but as I got closer I could feel his energy. He was not a body. He was more like a spirit or soul. We did not speak with our mouths, for he had no mouth. We spoke through our minds.

He showed me his planet. Then he took me to the Hall of Wisdom. It was made of crystal. It felt like the whole planet was inside a crystal. We talked about his planet and his people. He told me that they have existed for a long time because they didn't believe in destroying each other. They live together peacefully. I told him about my problems, about the bad things on Earth. And I told him I wanted to be like them: to live peacefully with no pain and no fear. And he told me rebirth is the secret. It's already in us and all we have to do is look inside us. All the answers are in us.

Then, all of a sudden, he had a bright ball in his hand and pointed at me. I felt cold and I started to shrink until I was small. Then he threw the ball through the wall and everything broke. All of a sudden I felt a warm glow all over my body. I saw a ball, it was full of color, it was like energy. I felt the energy go through my body. It was like taking a shower of light. It felt so peaceful. Antera told me that whenever I need an answer, all I have to do is look inside me because the answer will always be there.

—JENNIFER

At nineteen, Nelson surprised me by the clarity and depth of the insights from his inner journey. In three paragraphs and a drawing (figure C2-21), he summarizes profound truths contained in Eastern spiritual philosophies:

When asked to picture myself in a spaceship, I saw it form as an extension of my body. As I came upon the rainbow planet, I felt the force of gravity and motion, and coming into view of the surface I could see it all pass under me just like something out of Star Wars. Upon landing I noticed all the people were dressed in soft white and tan and brown robes. My blue loin cloth had developed into a blue stretch suit. I also had a sword scabbard on my back. These people were very friendly.

My guide took me all around the city and gave me several gifts, a hawk, a sword, a rose, and a book. These all had symbolic meaning. According to the various Eastern religions, there is a duality in the universe: dark and light, love and hate, sword and flower—In-Yo in Japanese, Uhm-Yang in Korean, and Yin/Yang in Chinese. The flower I received along with the sword represented these as separate entities, yet the hawk with both its power and grace was the fusion of these elements.

After the Yin and Yang are blended, a third state, Tao, or path, is achieved, where wisdom and spiritual unity replace emotional upheaval between two sides. For me, the book represented Tao as the final stage of spiritual development. Personally, these symbols also had to do with my own outlook. They meant there should be an intertwining between the warrior side of myself and the gentle side, both flowing into each other, neither dominating nor retreating, but existing and flourishing by augmenting what the other lacks.

—NELSON

Janet, along with other students in the class, knew that I was writing this book. Using a group visualization, the students imagined the book with their drawings and writings in it being out in the world, helping others release fears and reclaim their own creative powers. When Janet went on her inner journey to the Hall of Wisdom (figure C2-22) she was shown great books of the past as well as this book. I believe that this book finally became a reality as a result of the love, inner light, and wisdom of hundreds of people worldwide who worked together to visualize it as a reality. Janet relates her experience:

As I entered the House of Wisdom, I found myself surrounded by books. The first thing that caught my eye was the huge book on a stand in the middle of the room. I flipped through a few pages and realized that it was the Bible. My guide, Opus, told me that the best place to find the words of wisdom is in the Bible. I thanked him and began to read the passages he pointed out to me. Later on, I helped myself to some of the books in the bookcases. I found the complete collection of Shakespeare's work in the first bookcase. In the second, I found an entire selection of American and English literature. In the third, I found only a book with no title on it. My guide told me that this book was of great importance to me, to my classmates, and to my teacher. I opened the book and there weren't any words in it, but only a ray of rainbow colors coming directly to me. I closed the book, smiled at my guide, and assured him that this book would soon have a title and words.

—Janet

ACHIEVING ILLUMINED STATES OF INTUITION

In working through the exercises in this book, you developed your creative capacities and visual skills, and these together enabled you to experience deeper levels of spiritual truth. This project will help you to achieve illuminated states of intuition so you can access the wisdom within you. In chapters 1 and 5, you visualized yourself on the beautiful planet Earth, meeting a spiritual guide and your power animals. The visualization in this journey to the Hall of Wisdom and Higher Arts is different. You will stretch your imagination to reach the wisdom contained in other parts of the universe. Like my students, you'll meet a special spiritual guide who will lead you to the Hall of Wisdom and Higher Arts on another planet.

In your drawing, you will manifest visions you receive in this guided visualization. You will apply the elements of good design and the art skills you have learned in the previous chapters to create your own unique spiritual reality.

JOURNEY TO THE HALL OF WISDOM: A VISUALIZATION

It would be best to play the following visualization on a tape recorder, but you can also ask a friend to read it to you while playing soft, meditative music. The person who reads should go through the visualization slowly and pause at the ellipses (. . .) so you have time to see images. Remember to keep your mind and heart open while you go on this journey, and let your imagination flow unimpeded.

Before starting, place a piece of newsprint paper and a pencil next to you. As soon as you finish the guided visualization, quickly record your images and write in detail about your experiences and feelings, just as you did for your Power Animal Journey. If you have trouble recalling what you imagined, remain quiet and take yourself back on the journey.

Journey to the Hall of Wisdom
A VISUALIZATION

With your eyes closed, sit comfortably in a chair with your hands resting in your lap and your feet flat on the floor. Take a minute to recall the need for an open mind and heart to go on this journey. To do this, visualize your mind and heart expanding. Feel a lot of love and realize that you are wonderful. Imagine a ball or prism of rainbow light at the top of your head. Bring that energy down through your head into your brain, down along your spine into your lungs, and then into your heart. Let the light and love enter your heart. Now visualize it filling the room you are sitting in. See how far out you can push that energy. Bring that energy down through your stomach and into your other organs, down through your legs, and into the ground. Feel the stream of warm energy flowing from the top of your head all the way through your body and into the ground. Now guide the energy back up through your feet, along the back of your legs, and slowly up through your spine. Finally, bring it back into your head. Imagine a rainbow of energy spreading through your whole being—mind, body, and spirit.

Now you are ready for your journey to the Hall of Wisdom. Feel yourself lifting slowly and gently off the ground . . . Imagine you are floating in outer space. See the light and love of this cosmos filling your being. You are going on a fantastic voyage to a planet more highly evolved than our Earth. The people there are loving and peaceful . . . In your mind's eye create a spaceship to carry you there . . . Now imagine sitting inside your spaceship . . . Look out the window to view the galaxy. See the stars and the many brilliant planets and lights of this solar system . . . Imagine that your spaceship is traveling beyond the speed of light, leaving this galaxy behind to enter a strange new galaxy . . . As you enter a new galaxy, look out the window of your spaceship . . . You notice a large planet coming into view . . . The planet is surrounded in luminous rainbow lights . . . As your spaceship draws nearer, you begin to see the planet's landscape . . . In your imagination slow the speed of your spaceship. You are now ready to descend to this planet . . . See the landing strip below you . . . Now, slowly, gently, land your spacecraft there.

You are now safely landed on this rainbow planet. See yourself getting up from your seat on the ship and opening the door. Slowly you descend the landing ramp . . . There you see a group of warm and loving people who have come to greet you and welcome you to their planet. Open your heart and send a beam of love to them . . . Out of this crowd, one person starts walking toward you . . . This is your special friend and spirit guide who will show you around the city on this planet . . . As your special friend draws near you, introduce yourself and tell the guide your name. Listen as your guide tells you his or her name . . . With your heart open, send a beam of rainbow love to your guide. After you do this, you see and feel a beam of love coming from your guide directly to your heart.

Now that you and your guide have met and established a loving contact, you go with your guide toward the city . . . As you walk down the streets, notice what the buildings look like and how they are built . . . Notice what the people are wearing. What colors do you see in their clothing? . . . Do you see any flowers, trees, or animals? As you continue walking, you notice a special building ahead of you made of pure gold. Your guide tells you that this building is the Hall of Wisdom and Higher Arts . . . Your guide leads you toward the Hall of Wisdom.

Imagine yourself entering this building with your guide. As you go in, pay special attention to what is inside this Hall of Wisdom . . . Your guide is pointing out special things for you to see . . . Notice all the images that are shown to you . . .

Since this is the Hall of Wisdom, your guide has some special words of wisdom just for you. Listen and remember these words of wisdom . . . After listening, ask your guide for advice on any personal problems you are having or any fears you are experiencing . . .

Thank your guide for the words of wisdom and the advice.

Now it's time to leave the Hall of Wisdom . . . Look around once more at all the wonderful things you have seen. Then go with your guide out of the Hall of Wisdom and walk back into the city. Your guide leads you back down the streets to your spaceship's landing site. Before you go, embrace your guide and give thanks for all the gifts given to you. Say good-bye to your guide and to the wonderful people you have met. Then climb back into your spaceship.

Guiding your spaceship, you slowly lift off the ground . . . You are now in outer space heading toward Earth . . . On your journey homeward, recall in vivid detail all you have seen and heard so you can bring this information, these images, and your wisdom back to Earth.

Looking out the window of your spaceship, see the beautiful planet Earth looming into view—a powerful image of a swirling, radiant, blue pearl . . . As the planet comes closer into view, you can see the land and ocean underneath you. Gently, the ship slows down and starts its descent to the Earth . . . As the ship descends, recall the warm and loving feelings and images of your journey . . . Imagine now that your ship has landed on the ground . . . You are back home on Earth now. You are back in your room sitting in your chair . . . Slowly, when you are ready, open your eyes and in silence write and draw all that you have seen and heard.

PROJECT: DRAWING YOUR VISION

In chapter 5, you created a composition on newsprint paper made up of lines, shapes, and silhouettes of the images you saw on your Power Animal journey. You assembled these images, applying the elements of good design (pages 32–33). You will do the same for this project, using the images from your journey to the Hall of Wisdom.

The images you received may be totally new to you and unrelated to anything you see in your everyday world. Thus, you might not find any books or magazines you can use as resources in making your silhouette shapes. Trust your imagination, intuition, and drawing skills. You will find that you are able to draw what you saw. If you have any problems, return to the visualization and ask your special guide for help.

MATERIALS

- 2 sheets 18-by-24-inch newsprint paper
- 1 sheet 18-by-24-inch colored or black Canson paper (Canson papers come in an assortment of colors. Choose a color you like.)
- 1 large sheet white transfer paper
- 1 large sheet translucent tracing paper
- Scissors
- # 2 pencil
- Eraser
- Pencil sharpener
- Ruler
- Small roll of masking tape
- Inspirational music
- Bristol Prisma colored pencils

# 905 aquamarine	# 938 white
# 930 magenta	# 910 true green
# 903 true-blue	# 923 scarlet lake
# 913 green	# 933 blue-violet
# 918 orange	# 935 black
# 932 violet	
# 916 canary yellow	

- The following are optional prisma colors:

# 904 light blue	# 956 light violet
# 939 flesh	# 934 lavender
# 929 pink	# 928 blush

- An audio tape of the guided visualization used for this chapter is available. See the Appendix.

PROCEDURES

1. Gather the images you drew, newsprint paper, a pencil, scissors, ruler, eraser, and a sheet of tracing paper. On the newsprint paper, measure and draw a 16-by-20-inch rectangle. (This format size is only suggested. Feel free to create any format size and shape that fits your vision.)

2. Before you begin, turn to chapter 5, Drawing from Your Inner Vision. Review procedures 1 through 7 under this heading. Then begin constructing your line drawing, following the procedures outlined.

3. When you have completed your line drawing, take out your black paper, white transfer paper, and a roll of tape. Then go back to part 2 of chapter 5 for instructions on transferring your drawing to black paper.

4. Now take out your colored pencils. Review the color-mixing procedures by turning to part 1 of chapter 5. Before you begin coloring your final vision, it is essential to repeat the guided visualization for the Hall of Wisdom. This will enable you to work freely and confidently.

5. As you are coloring your drawing, think of your colors as radiant light and know that the vision you are manifesting is your unique light, love, color, and truth.

6. As you work on your drawing, you may find the vision changing from what you remember seeing. It is a natural part of the creative process. Give your imagination the freedom to expand the concept as you go. Above all, follow your heart; realize that power and knowledge are within you.

WHAT HAVE YOU LEARNED?

In doing this project, you used your creative power to go beyond ordinary reality and uncover insights into problems or fears that you may be facing either in your art or in your life. You learned that you have answers within you to help solve any problems, including how to create peace in the world. The fact that you could imagine peace on another planet means that peace is already a possibility. Making this peace a reality on earth is like your drawing inner visions: It requires only your committed effort, love, and innate wisdom. Peace starts within yourself. When you attain inner peace, you add peace to the world.

Although you have completed all the projects in this book, do not consider yourself finished—you are beginning. The exercises in this book are open-ended because your creativity is unlimited. You could start the projects all over again, and with the knowledge, skills, and insights you've gained, you will create inspirational images that go beyond your first accomplishments.

The creative process works like the seed of a flower warmed by the sun: The more you open yourself to the light within you, the more fully and radiantly your creative energy will blossom. Like all of nature, your nature is to grow, evolve, and create. In tapping your inner powers you are laying claim to that part of yourself that is divine because it can create beauty, truth, and light out of nothingness. By expressing your inner light, you reconnect with a "higher Light beyond darkness":

Beholding the higher Light beyond the darkness we came to the Divine Sun in the Godhead, to the highest Light of all.
—RIG VEDA I.50.10

SUGGESTED READING

Hall, Manly P. *The Secret Teachings of All Ages.* Los Angeles: Philosophical Research Society, 1977.

Harman, Willis, and Howard Reingold. *Higher Creativity.* Los Angeles: J. P. Tarcher, 1984.

Head, Joseph, and S. L. Cranston. *Reincarnation: The Phoenix Fire Mystery.* New York: Julian Press/Crown Publishers, 1977.

Huffines, LeUna. *Bridge of Light: Tools of Light for Transformation.* New York: Simon & Schuster, 1989.

Piper, Raymond F. and Lila K. Piper. *Cosmic Art.* New York: Hawthorn Books, 1975.

Ridall, Kathryn. *Channeling: How to Reach Out to Your Spirit Guides.* New York: Bantam Books, 1988.

Roman, Sanaya, and Duane Packer. *Opening to Channel: How to Connect with Your Spirit Guide.* Tiburon, Calif.: H. J. Kramer, 1987.

Yatri. *Unknown Man: The Mysterious Birth of a New Species.* New York: Simon & Schuster, 1988.

NOTES

1. David V. Erdman, *The Poetry and Prose of William Blake* (New York: Doubleday, 1982).

CHAPTER 7

Birthing a New Renaissance

We shall require a substantially new manner of thinking if mankind is to survive.

—Albert Einstein

. . . in your own Bosom you bear your Heaven and Earth, & all you behold, tho it appears Without, it is Within, In your Imagination . . .

—William Blake[1]

*When Imaginative Art & Science & all Intellectual Gifts
all Gifts of the Holy Ghost are looked upon as of no use & only Contention
remains to Man the Last Judgement begins & its Vision is seen
by the (Imaginative Eye) of Everyone according to the situation he holds.*

—William Blake[2]

IF YOU HAVE completed the projects in this book, you will already have acquired what Einstein calls a "substantially new manner of thinking": new ways of seeing and new ways of creating. You learned these new orientations to life by changing your mental focus to inner light and integrating the functions of logic and reason with intuition and imagination. Through this process you also discovered that you are a being with potent creative powers.

Through guided visualizations, you learned to perceive in new ways. You also learned that you have the power to tap the wisdom within yourself and make sacred connections with all life forms. You recognized that there are no such things as black, white, and gray, but rather a colorful flow of life, light, and energy. You acquired basic art skills and learned the elements of good design that empower you to create your own visions of beauty, harmony, and light. You can manifest internal visions in the physical world. Knowing this, it becomes clear that you can play a cocreative role in making the world what it is.

EXPANDING YOUR CONCEPT OF ARTIST

This book has led you through the visual practices of drawing and painting, but don't let it limit your concept of what art is or what it means to be an artist. *An artist is one who has the ability to create.* As you have learned, every human being has this ability to create and imagine at some level, so don't narrow your definition of an artist to professional painters, sculptors, musicians, or writers. You can apply the creative problem-solving skills you gained from this book to any field, be it medicine, psychology, science, economics, technology, architecture, or clothing design. You can even use it to enrich and re-create your relationships.

In this way, you, I, and every other individual in the world today is contributing to the present state of the Earth. War, nuclear weapons, poverty, pollution, economic imbalance, social inequality, breakthroughs in medicine, advances in technology, incredible inventions, and beautiful designs are all the result of our mind's creations and the focus of our collective imagination. When our imagination is rooted in fear, lack of love, and distrust of our own creative power to heal discord, we tend to seek solutions outside of ourselves and blame others. As Einstein noted, we need our "new manner of thinking" for the present age.

PLAYING A COCREATIVE ROLE

We have grown up thinking that art and the act of creating are separate from science; that science is separate from spiritual practices; that spiritual practices are separate from the creative powers of the mind; that the creative powers of the mind are separate from and do not affect physical matter. In a new and broader understanding of what it means to be an artist, however, art, science, and ancient wisdom begin to merge into a rich composite with new meaning for us. The new image of humanity emerging in our century is that of the divine artist in everyone: We are each cocreators in a collective vision of the universe. Illumined by the brilliant possibilities opened by the atomic age, this vision shines on all of us, beaming the truth of our potent godlike natures. In many spiritual traditions, this godlike aspect of humanity is revered and attainable. Yet for many of us, reaching our godly potential seems a remote possibility.

In this book you learned about both inner and outer light. Light and energy is the unifying element in art, science, and all spiritual traditions. Mystical teachings through the ages say that we are all one in mind, body, and spirit. Proof of our physical oneness in visible light and other electromagnetic energies has come within our century from studies in astro and subatomic physics. Scientists have discovered what wise people have always known: that you and I partake of the same visible light and that the atomic structures that make up our physical bodies shared their beginnings in some past stellar explosion. Thus, your body shares the atoms of the earth and the rays of the sun. This energy binds you and me together along with all other forms of life in an unbroken web: We are a physical unity of bioelectromagnetic energy. Spiritual unity, however—the ultimate reality of our oneness—is comprehended only when you see with the eye of contemplation past the limits of culture, ritual, logic, and physical perception to the inner light that is in all of us.

DARING TO BRING YOUR LIGHT AND LOVE TO THE WORLD

If you feel fragmented, fearful, or aggressive, realize that these feelings are a result of how you focus your mind and creative energies. You have within you the power to feel complete, fearless, and at peace. It takes courage to be fully who you are; to become the integrated artist that you are meant to be; to think, act, and create with responsibility beyond the narrow limits you have been taught to accept. Dare to bring your light, love, and vision to the world. What you create through the divine powers of your imagination affects the whole world. Manifest each day your healing gifts of beauty, peace, and harmony. As you raise your level of inner light and joy, you will play a significant role in the birth of the New Renaissance—a *light* that is already dawning. It is a new light illuminating a new world, born of the power and greatness within all of us.

NOTES

1. David V. Erdman, *The Poetry and Prose of William Blake* (New York: Doubleday, 1965), 223.
2. Ibid, 544.

AFTERWORD: CREATING INSPIRED WORKS USING THE COMPUTER

Spirit is the light of the soul. Spirit is the creative energy of the Cosmos. The soul of man is not conscious of its powers until it is enlightened by Spirit. Therefore, to evolve and grow, man must learn how to use and develop his own soul forces. . .

—Johannes Brahms[1]

All true art is an expression of the soul. The outward forms have value only in so far as they are expressions of the inward spirit of man. . . Whenever men begin to see Beauty in Truth, then true art will arise.

—Mahatma Gandhi[2]

You can infuse your designs with the light of your soul using a computer or any other media, if you are willing to practice patiently and pray deeply to be inspired. When creating with a computer, remember that like paints, pencils, and all objects of the phenomenal universe, a computer is a device molded from fluid electromagnetic energies which can become saturated with your consciousness.

THE COMPUTER: A MIRROR OF CONSCIOUSNESS

Today many people are beginning to use the computer as a creative medium. The computer is a mirror that makes visible our invisible thoughts by projecting them onto a vibrant, phosphorescent screen. When you turn on the computer, its musical sounds gradually increase in vibration until, like magic, the monitor lights up with activated photons of light.

As a tool for creative work and for communication, the computer is more powerful and more versatile than the paints and pencils you used in earlier chapters. When we enter our thoughts into the computer, they become symbols—images, mathematical equations, music, and words—forged in light.

Thought is the primary energy and vibration that emanated from God and is thus the creator of life, electrons, atoms, and all forms of energy. Thought itself is the finest vibratory energy, the speediest power among all powers.

—Paramahansa Yogananda[3]

The computer can receive, store, and transmit these symbols around the world at the speed of light. Today millions of ordinary people are sitting in front of computers with the technological capacity to create images and words that can be transmitted in bytes of light and sound to other people through e-mail and the Internet. The mirror effect of sending one person's thoughts or graphic images around the globe, multiplied by millions of people, amplifies exponentially the power of the computer to imprint positive or negative thought vibrations through cyberspace onto the collective consciousness.

GARBAGE IN—GARBAGE OUT

The computer itself does not create great art nor a great computer-linked world culture. Computers are tools; their impact is determined by the thoughts each user encodes. Thoughts are energy, more subtle than electromagnetic energies. Projected as images, sounds, and words, thoughts have the power to demoralize or edify humanity. We each have been given the free will to create images of destruction that instill fear, hatred, anger, and greed. Or, we are free to create from inspired ideas that reflect the essential beauty and luminosity of the soul. A powerful computer will not in itself help you create radiant images of inner light; you must also open your heart to love and perceive yourself and others as souls who are one with Spirit.

INSPIRATION AND INNER LIGHT

In her excellent book *The Fiery Muse*, Teri Degler writes about what the great music composer Johannes Brahms told a young interviewer named Abell about his experience with divine inspiration.

Before beginning to compose, Degler writes, Brahms' first step was to contemplate the awesome realization that we are one with God. He would then "appeal directly to the Creator and ask what he felt were three of the most seminal philosophical questions concerning human existence: whence *(woher)*, wherefore *(warum)*, whither *(wohin)*? When this was completed, he would begin to feel vibrations that would thrill his whole being. These vibrations, he said, were 'the Spirit illuminating the soul-power within'."

Brahms went on to describe in detail the process of divine inspiration: "Those vibrations assume the forms of distinct mental images, after I have formulated my desire and resolve in regard to what I want, namely, to be inspired so that I can compose something that will uplift and benefit humanity, something of permanent value. . . . Straightway the ideas flow in upon me, directly from God, and not only do I see distinct themes in my mind's eye, but they are clothed in the right forms, harmonies, and orchestration. Measure by measure, the finished product is revealed to me. . . ."[4]

Johannes Brahms is a shining example of a spiritual genius who made a great and lasting contribution to the world. To follow his example of responsible creativity, you can use the following blessing for the computer and prayer for inspiration anytime you sit down to use this powerful medium.

The soul created the arts wherever they have flourished. . .

Insist on yourself; never imitate. Your own gift you can present every moment with the cumulative force of a whole life's cultivation; but of the adopted talent of another, you have only an extemporaneous half-possession. That which each can do best, none but his Maker can teach him.

—Ralph Waldo Emerson[5]

MEDITATION: BLESSING THE COMPUTER

When I set up my new computer, I scanned into it a number of pictures of saints and sages who inspire and guide me. They sit as small icons on my computer desktop. You also might want to add sacred images to your computer desktop to help make your workspace sacred. Here is a blessing ritual you can do before you use the computer to create.

With your computer turned on, sit in front of it with your hands on the keyboard, your eyes slightly closed, and your attention focused in the third or spiritual eye in the middle of your forehead. If you wish, soft inspirational or sacred music can be playing in the background.

Gently quiet your breathing. Keeping your heart receptive, imagine in your spiritual eye your favorite saint or sage — or just pure white Light of Consciousness—as being radiantly present and full of blessing for you.

Visualize that blessing light as shining from the spiritual eye into your heart, filling you with a warm feeling of unconditional love. Direct the light from your heart to all the organs, cells, and atoms of your body. When your whole body is filled with light, direct the light to flow through your arms into your hands and fingertips.

Then visualize the light flowing from your hands and fingertips into the keyboard blessing the computer. Imagine this blessing light impregnating and spiritualizing all the atoms and molecules of the computer.

PRAYER FOR INSPIRATION

Be clear about your creative objectives. You can modify the prayer that follows to ask for inspiration for whatever specific project you are working on.

Sit with your back straight facing the computer. With your attention focused in the heart, bring back the feeling of the blessing light and unconditional love of God flowing within you. Pause in meditative silence until you experience this sensation.

With as much devotion and attunement to God as you can muster, begin the following prayer: "Divine Mother, Father God, inspire and guide me always. Help me to remember that as a soul, I am always one with You. Illumine and inspire my heart and mind to bring forth [a design, computer generated painting, poem, book, musical composition, or scientific invention] that is uplifting and beneficial to humanity. Help me to overcome fear so that I can manifest lovingly and courageously my soul's creative gifts of beauty, truth, and light and be a beacon of hope and inspiration to others."

When you have finished your prayer, wait in silence for that subtle energy of inspiration to bubble up in your heart. Keep perfectly relaxed while waiting for images to arise in the mind.

When you receive an image, place it in your heart and, giving thanks to God, surround it with the light of unconditional love.

Holding to your inner vision and with heartfelt enthusiasm, begin using the computer to create. Every time you feel stuck, relax and ask God to guide you.

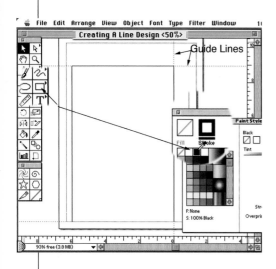

Figure A-1. Open the Adobe Illustrator program. Under the File menu, choose Document Set Up. Change the Ruler Units to inches and click the OK button.

Under the File menu, select Save. Title and save your document to the desktop.

Set up guidelines for a six-inch wide by nine-inch tall rectangle as a format to frame your line design.

Next select the Paint Dropper and place the color black in the stroke box. Make sure the Fill box has not been selected. Select the Rectangle tool and create an outline using the six-by-nine rule lines to guide you.

PROJECT 1: CREATING A LINE DESIGN USING A COMPUTER

This project is based on understanding the elements of good design and the "gray scale" as a "scale of light" as presented in Chapter 1. If you are not familiar with these concepts, review them before beginning. This exercise also assumes that you have basic computer skills and access to a computer powerful enough to run graphics programs.

I have often been asked to teach people how to create luminous images like the one on the cover of this book. I have discovered there are many ways to create luminous art using the computer. The following is but *one* fairly simple technique that should provide successful results even years from now, despite changes in software and computer technology. Once you feel comfortable with the process as outlined here, explore other ways of creating luminous images as illustrated in software manuals and books on the subject.

The secret to using the computer to create is to begin with inspired vision, consciously incorporating the principles of good design. Then the computer and its ever more powerful programs are simply better tools to manifest your inner vision. When I am stuck in my creative process, I ask God and the Great Ones to guide me. To my astonishment and delight, I have been guided in how to do things on the computer that are not in the software manuals! Have no doubt, the Divine Artist who continually creates the universe is infinitely capable of understanding the intricacies of the computer.

MATERIALS

If you're planning to create many luminous graphics, you should invest in the fastest computer within your budget. To create the cover art, chapter openers, and illustrations in this chapter, I used a Macintosh Power PC 7600/120, running Adobe Photoshop 3.0.5 and Adobe Illustrator 6.0. Technology is advancing so rapidly that you may be using an even faster computer and more powerful programs. Therefore the following are suggested guidelines only.

Hardware: A Power PC computer with at least 16 MB of RAM and 1-gigabyte of hard drive memory. 40 or more MB of RAM is preferable for using the Photoshop program.

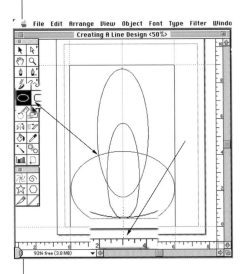

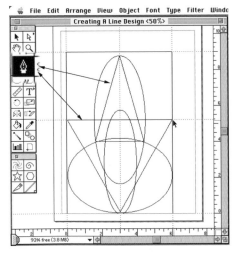

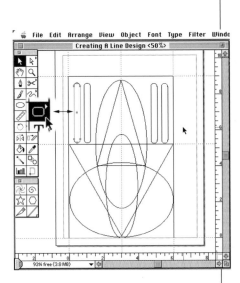

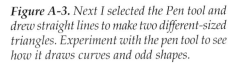

Figure A-2. *To illustrate basic design principles outlined in Chapter 1, I made a bilateral symmetrical design. I placed a rule guide at the three-inch mark to divide the rectangle in half vertically.*

Then I selected the Oval tool and experimented with creating various sizes of ovals, lining each up on the middle guideline. Experiment with the Oval tool; it also can draw precise circles.

Figure A-3. *Next I selected the Pen tool and drew straight lines to make two different-sized triangles. Experiment with the pen tool to see how it draws curves and odd shapes.*

Figure A-4. *Next I selected the Rounded Corner Rectangle tool and made a series of four rectangles by creating one and then duplicating it three times. Placing two on each side of the guide line completed the symmetrical design.*

Next I opened the Photoshop program and imported the Illustrator file into it to illuminate my design (see figures A-7 through A-12).

Software: The latest versions of Adobe Photoshop and Adobe Illustrator.
Drawing the Light From Within guided visualization tapes (see Resources, page 211).
Inspirational music.

PROCEDURES

1. Open your Adobe Illustrator program and set up a new document as outlined in Figure A-1.
2. Study figures A-2 through A-4 to see how I created a line design. Then reread *Creating A Line Design For Your Painting,* Chapter 1, page 30. When experimenting with a line design, you do not need to use the drawing tools in the same order as I did. Allow your inner voice and intuition to guide you.

3. After practicing techniques and familiarized yourself with the Illustrator drawing tools, do the *Prayer for Inspiration* on page 203.

4. When you receive an image, open a new Illustrator page and begin creating from your inner vision using the principles of good design. You may want to play some inspirational music while you are working. When you feel complete with your design, save it, and proceed to Project 2.

PROJECT 2: CREATING A SCALE OF LIGHT USING PHOTOSHOP

In Chapter 1 you created a scale of light with paint that had nine gradations going from black to white. The Photoshop program automatically creates 250 gradations, making it easy for anyone to create a smooth luminous transition from black to white light.

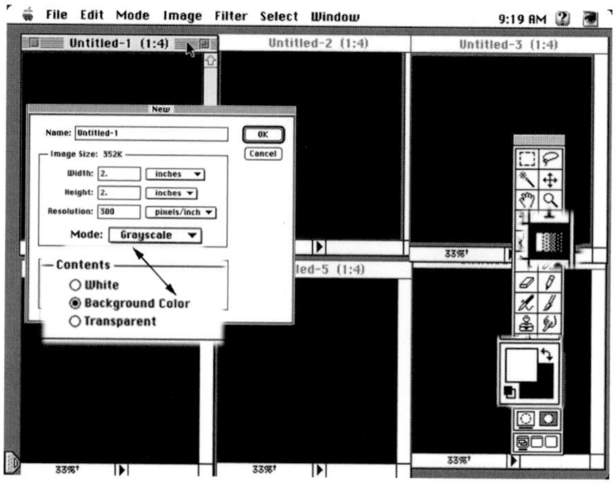

Figure A-5. First I went to File menu, clicked on New, and filled in the specifications for a two-by-two-inch format having a black background, set to gray scale mode. I created six new documents in this way and lined them up in two rows on my desktop.

Next, I clicked on the Gradient tool (the one that looks like a gray scale image) and experimented with the tool as illustrated in figure A-6.

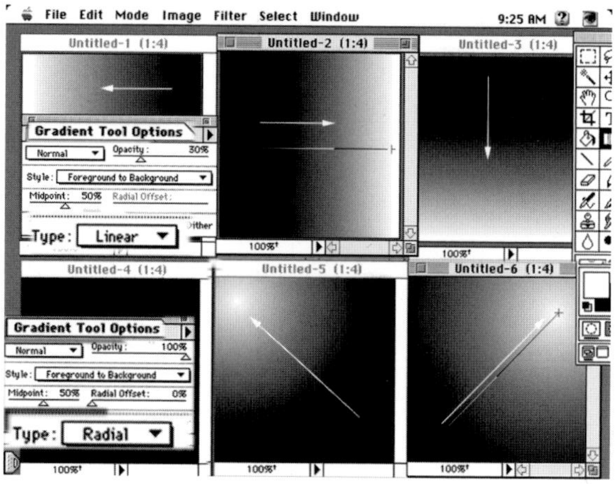

Figure A-6. Double clicking on the Gradient tool popped up the options. I chose Type as Linear and Style as Foreground to Background.

In the top row I created linear gradations of light by dragging the tool from left to right or from top to bottom using parallel horizontal and vertical movements.

In the bottom row I set the Gradient tool Type to Radial, keeping the Style as Foreground to Background. I dragged the pointer from a corner or out from the center of a document to create light radiating in circles from a central point.

PROCEDURES

1. Using figure A-5 as a guide, open your Photoshop program and set up six new documents with a black background approximately two inches by two inches in size. Set the documents to gray scale mode. Line the documents up in two rows so that you can see them all at once.
2. Study figure A-6 to understanding how to use the gradient tool to create linear and circular scales of light.
3. Then begin experimenting in your own documents to create blends of light. When you are familiar with using the gradient tool, proceed to Project 3.

PROJECT 3: BRINGING RADIANCE TO YOUR DESIGN

PROCEDURES

1. Study the captions under figures A-7 through A-12 to help you understand the steps you will take to make your design luminous.
2. Click on the word Open in the Photoshop File menu. Retrieve the line design you created in Adobe Illustrator in Project 1.
3. Use the magic wand to select part of the design. Go to the menu bar under Edit and choose Fill. Fill the selected section with either a black foreground or white background color (see figures A-7 and A-8). After you have finished, say once again the *Prayer For Inspiration.*
4. With an inspired heart, use the magic wand to select one area at a time and use the gradient tool to create a radial or linear illumination in each section (see figures A-9 and A-10).
5. When you finish, go the menu bar under Filters and select Gaussian Blur. This procedure smoothes the edges of your design.
6. Then go to Select on the menu bar and click on Select All. Then go to Edit and select Copy (see figures A-11 and A-12).
7. Go to the File menu and select New to create a new Photoshop document the same size as your imported Illustrator document. Go to the Edit menu and select Paste. This will paste a

Figure A-7. With the Photoshop program open, I went to the menu bar under File and clicked Open. Then I went to my computer desktop and clicked on the Adobe Illustrator line design. I used the Magic Wand tool to select part of the design.

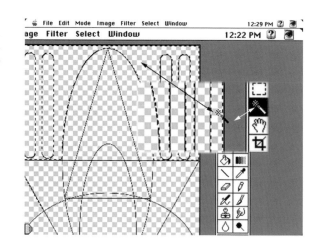

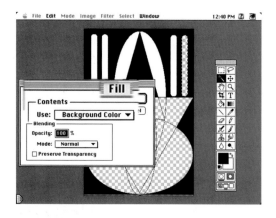

Figure A-8. Next I went to the menu bar under Edit, chose Fill, and selected Use Background color. This filled the selected area with black.

Using the Magic Wand, I selected a different area, chose Fill, and selected Use Foreground color. This filled the selected area with white.

I continued alternating the Fills until each area was filled with black or white color.

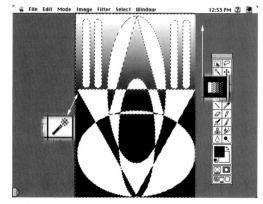

Figure A-9. Then I used the Magic Wand to select the largest black-colored section of the design.

Clicking on the Gradient tool set to Linear mode, I pulled the mouse in a vertical direction from top to bottom creating a linear scale of light in the selected area.

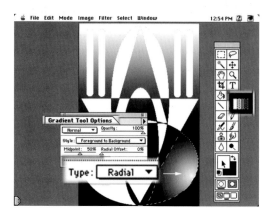

Figure A-10. In some of the selected areas, I double-clicked on the Gradient tool and set the Type to Radial so that the light in that section would proceed outward from the center of a circle. Experiment with the many ways of creating light. Choose a method that enhances the luminosity of each section of the design you have created.

copy of the Illustrator image into a Photoshop file. Name the new document and save it as a tiff or eps file. The new Photoshop document can be imported into a layout program which you can print out later.

Every exercise in this book can be done using the computer. I suggest that you practice creating many asymmetrical and symmetrical line designs. Then import the most exciting and inspiring designs into Photoshop and illuminate them. As you become more proficient in using graphic programs, try using the computer to complete other exercises in the book.

ETHICS OF THE SOUL

Today the computer makes it easier than ever to copy and modify another person's work. You are a unique and radiant soul—you do not need to copy anyone else's gifts. Nothing is impossible to the artist who realizes a connection with God. You have been endowed with the DNA of spiritual genius from the greatest Artist of all—your Divine Mother/Father God. Move beyond limiting beliefs and negativity by striving courageously to bless the world with the blossoms of your soul's original beauty, harmony, and truth.

Light is the matrix of material and spiritual reality. Millions of atomic suns shine in your computer waiting for you to use them to create. All Great Ones leave luminous soul prints in the sands of time that glorify God and edify all humanity. Imagine how much better the world would be if you left yours.

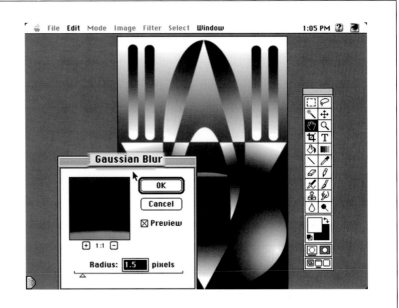

Figure A-11. After bringing radiance to the design, I went to the Menu bar, chose Filter, and clicked on Gaussian Blur to smooth any rough pixel edges in the design.

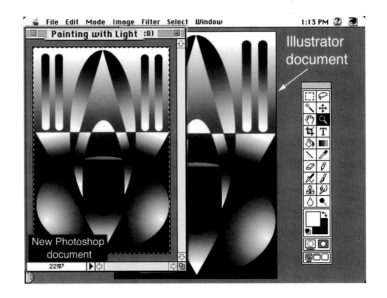

Figure A-12. Finally, I opened a new document in Photoshop and titled it Painting With Light.

Next I switched back to the Illustrator and on the menu bar under Select, clicked on Select All to select the whole Illustrator file.

Then under Edit, I selected Copy. I clicked on the document titled Painting With Light and Pasted and Saved the new document as a tiff file to be used later in other programs.

SUGGESTED READING

Cornell, Judith. *MANDALA: Luminous Symbols for Healing*. Wheaton, Ill.: Quest Books, 1994.

Degler, Teri. *The Fiery Muse: Creativity and the Spiritual Quest*. Toronto: Random House of Canada, 1996.

Phillips, Jan. *Marry Your Muse: Making a Lasting Commitment to Your Creativity*. Wheaton, Ill.: Quest Books, 1997.

NOTES

1. Arthur Abell, *Talks with Great Composers* (New York: Philosophical Library, 1995) as quoted in Teri Degler, *The Fiery Muse: Creativity and the Spiritual Quest* (Toronto: Random House of Canada, 1996), 63-64.

2. Mahatma Gandhi, *Mohan-Mala: A Gandhian Rosary* (Ahmedabad: Navajivan Publishing, 1991), 115-116.

3. Paramahansa Yoganada, *God Talks with Arjuna, The Bhagavad Gita: Royal Science of God-Realization* (Los Angeles: Self-Realization Fellowship, 1995), 648.

4. Extracted from *The Fiery Muse* by Teri Degler. Copyright © 1995. Reprinted by permission of Random House of Canada Limited, 64.

5. Ralph Waldo Emerson, *Selected Essays* (New York: Penguin Classics, 1985), 198-199.

APPENDIX: SUGGESTED RESOURCES

The following resources will further facilitate your efforts in manifesting your creative gifts and unique healing light in the world.

DRAWING THE LIGHT FROM WITHIN (audio tapes)

Audio cassette tapes of the visualizations and meditations in this book are now available. These special meditations set to music gently guide you through the creative exercises in this book.

This two-cassette album is $19.95 plus $3.00 shipping. California residents add 7.25% sales tax; Canada and Mexico orders add $2.00 to shipping; overseas orders add $8.00 to shipping. Send check or Money Order (U.S. funds only) payable to:

> MANIFESTING INNER LIGHT
> P.O. BOX 517
> Sausalito, CA 94966-0517

MANDALA: LUMINOUS SYMBOLS FOR HEALING (book)
by Judith Cornell

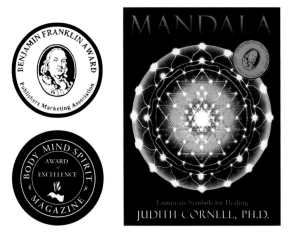

MANDALA (Quest Books, 1994), winner of the 1995 Benjamin Franklin Award for publishing excellence and the 1996 *Body, Mind, Spirit* Book Award, presents the art of the mandala as a self-empowering approach to well-being and self-knowledge. Simple exercises teach you to create mandalas for healing body, mind, and spirit. Oversize, full-color ($25.95). Available at bookstores or by mail order from the publisher. For ordering information, call:

> Quest Books
> Wheaton, Illinois
> (800) 669-9425

MANDALA: LUMINOUS SYMBOLS FOR HEALING (audio tapes)
by Judith Cornell

Quest Books has produced special audio cassette tapes of the meditations included in the book. These recorded meditations set to music guide you easily through the healing exercises in the book. Two-tape cassette set ($16.00) is available at bookstores or by mail order from the publisher. For ordering information, call:

> Quest Books
> Wheaton, Illinois
> (800) 669-9425

MANIFESTING INNER LIGHT (organization)

Founded in 1987 by Judith Cornell, this organization is dedicated to merging sacred art, science, and ancient wisdom. It maintains a mailing list and sends out newsletters with information about Judith's scheduled seminars and lectures and a catalog listing tapes, books, videos, and music to use with DRAWING THE LIGHT FROM WITHIN or MANDALA.

To reach Judith or add your name to the mailing list, contact:

> MANIFESTING INNER LIGHT
> P.O. BOX 517
> Sausalito, CA 94966-0517
> (415) 332-4663 or E-mail ommandala@aol.com

QUEST BOOKS
are published by
The Theosophical Society in America,
Wheaton, Illinois 60189-0270,
a branch of a world organization
dedicated to the promotion of the unity of
humanity and the encouragement of the study of
religion, philosophy, and science, to the end that
we may better understand ourselves and our place in
the universe. The Society stands for complete
freedom of individual search and belief.
For further information about its activities,
write, call 1-800-669-1571, or consult its Web page:
http://www.theosophical.org

The Theosophical Publishing House
is aided by the generous support of
THE KERN FOUNDATION,
a trust established by Herbert A. Kern
and dedicated to Theosophical education.